*Earn good money doing what you love
and still have time to play*

Build A 6 Figure Product Business

HEATHER KATSONGA-WOODWARD

Founder of  **Queen** of **Kinks, Curls & Coils**®

FOREWORD BY BUSHRA AZHAR

RETHINK PRESS

First published in Great Britain 2015
by Rethink Press (www.rethinkpress.com)

© Copyright Heather Katsonga Woodward

CONTENTS

FOREWORD

Heather is giving me a dream, but unlike all the other self-help business books, this dream comes with a full how-to manual... and guess what? The manual is one of the best I have ever come across.

The nerd in me loves that there is a model; the concept of *The Money Spot*™ is not just a pie-in-the-sky fluffy idea. It is a strategic concept that not only makes total sense to my accountant brain but is also easy to grasp for those who are not proficient in management theory. Breaking down the model further into bite-sized chunks that are also highly actionable makes it incredibly easy for anyone to follow it, even without any prior business knowledge.

Another great thing about *The Money Spot*™ is that you will see case studies and anecdotes of people just like you sprinkled throughout the book. These stories aren't just there for entertainment, they are there to kick your butt into gear, to see yourself in those situations and think to yourself, 'Oh, so this is how you get out of that sticky situation or negative thought pattern.'

The 3-step blueprint on how to transition from your day job into a full-time, highly lucrative business is not only highly practical, but also takes the overwhelm out of the decision.

I have zero cosmetic capability (or inclination) but I understand business and Heather's tips on marketing, producing and promoting your products are spot on for any business. Because she has lived the experience of doing it in a beauty business, if I were to start a beauty business, I would just follow all her tips without question.

The chapter titled 'Get Into Specialist Stores and Specialist Locations' gives you a foolproof formula on how you can break free from the curse of The Mass (supermarkets) and get into the premier league of beauty products – because that's where the real money is. This is advice that I wish more authors gave in their books; when it comes to products, your positioning is what matters most and if you manage to get that right, you can command any price.

Lastly, I want to talk about the section on negotiation and selling in *The Money Spot*™. This is an area where I consider myself quite proficient and scoff at most guru advice. I am happy to report that Heather has managed to cover this area beautifully with specific, actionable takeaways that not only work but are also super easy to implement.

I hope you enjoy this book as much as I did and if you are considering starting a product business, this should be your first stop. If you are already running a product business, this book will give you insights and tactics that will help catapult your business to an entirely new level.

All my best wishes

Bushra Azhar
Founder, The Persuasion Revolution

INTRODUCTION

If you think back to high school and look at the people you were surrounded by, you can probably identify the one or two high performers who were bound to be running a profitable beauty business one day: they were smart as well as pretty and always on-trend. I wasn't one of those girls, and yet, here I am.

Smart? I certainly was, but I could hardly be bothered to change out of uniform on most days and as soon as I made prefect, I never did. I was in boarding school from the age of 11 and if you went back and asked most people, *what do you think Heather's future career will be?* they would likely have placed me in something sober and straight-laced like banking or law.

That is indeed where I started. The first seven years of my career were spent across two investment banks. It was a worthwhile life experience, but the daily grind of a regular job wasn't the lifestyle I wanted.

I know you can probably relate to some, if not all, of the issues that I had:

I really enjoyed my job and I got along well with my colleagues but I began to dread Sundays – the thought of having to wake up early for work the next day plagued me. I suffered from insomnia at times, but I still had to show up for work at the same time each day; now, I can have a lie in and work my schedule around my day. There is no way you can work well if you haven't slept well, but regular jobs don't take these life events into account.

I hated having to work from the office when I felt like working from home or a café – now I work from whatever café or even country I feel like being in at that time. Yes, even sellers of physical products can do that in this world of highly developed third-party services.

As an employee I felt guilty about taking time off for hospital visits – I felt that even if my manager understood he would probably prefer me to be working. I remember one awkward morning when he asked why I had needed to see my doctor. I replied, 'I have polycystic ovaries and my menstrual period was out of whack.'

'Why the hell are you telling me that for?' he asked, flabbergasted by my female issues.

'Well, you asked!'

The truth is the truth after all; whether someone wants to hear it is another matter.

Worst of all, I saw how every parent around me was sacrificing time with their kids for money. This isn't limited to high status careers; oh no, even if you're working in a factory your life is inflexible. You have to take your kids to a carer first thing in the morning to get into work. You see them for a couple of miserable hours at night when you're both tired. At times, you have to work weekends, losing family time that can never be recouped. I had no kids myself at the time but I could sympathize with all these problems my colleagues told me about.

I was certain this was not the life I wanted for myself. I created a strategy in 2009 that had me out of full-time work by 2012. I quit my job in investment banking to start a coaching business. Six months into that, I realized I was going nowhere and it was time to pivot, fast.

As my savings were running dry, I asked myself a few central questions:
How can I build a six-figure product business from home? I don't want to make the products myself and I want someone

else to post and pack orders for me so that I can spend more time with my family. I also don't want to pay too much for these services.

Indeed, there is a large and growing niche of women who are stuck in the rat race and fervently wish they had more control over their lives. They want to spend more time with their families and enjoy a lifestyle of their choosing.

Many of these women have a hobby or passion involving a craft (knitting, sewing, DIY upholstery) or beauty (hair, makeup or fashion) or some other product they fashion with their hands. A small number monetize this interest with some cottage industry and although they could build a huge brand and business around it – they simply have no idea how to, nor that it is even possible.

I personally have several friends in this category. They see small businesses grow from social media success but they never think that this could be them.

The Money Spot™ Program on How To Build A Six-Figure Product Business is unique in that it provides an easy-to-follow framework for building a big brand and business. The book is very current; it explores some tools that are not well known such as contract manufacturing and order fulfillment houses as well as social media tools that people use daily for personal reasons but are not sure how to use for business. The entire book is based on my own experience in building a six-figure hair product business.

I was interested in hair at the time I decided to change from coaching, but knew nothing about it. All I knew was that I wanted to be an authority on the subject. The biggest kinky and curly hair blog at that time already had 183,000 Facebook fans and there was a new hair blogger cropping up every single day. My strategy was simple: produce high quality content, prolifically.

As I had failed to grow two other businesses, my expectations were low. All I knew was that I did not want to be an employee again. I needed to make this work.

The response astounded me. A year and a half later, I had well over 300,000 Facebook fans and an email list of about 30,000 subscribers.

You can trust what I have to say because I have done it myself. I'm not particularly slim and averagely attractive, so looks are thankfully not a prerequisite for success in building a beauty brand. Indeed, the principles in this book can be applied to most products. In addition, when I launched into the beauty business, my savings were running out, so having lots of money is not a requirement either.

I worked on my own but I had an army behind me: third party manufacturers and a fulfillment house. They made my products, packed and shipped orders to my customers and brought my ideas to life.

This all sounds too good to be true, I know, but it really happened to me. You see, whilst my initial strategy was to simply produce content over time, I strategically added to that plan, and ended up with what I now call *The Money Spot*™ model. It is a three-part framework that shows how **Branding, Marketing and Distribution** can be optimized to create a lasting and fast-growing brand.

For most people the prospect of starting a business is daunting. Where do you start? How do you convince other people to help you? You don't feel you're credible; you don't feel you have something to offer that isn't already out there; you don't know how to get people to follow you and can't figure out why no one is engaging with your content. You think it's too risky – I certainly had all these fears.

Too scared to take action, most people never get past fantasizing about what life would be like if they could set the pace. Eventually, the difference between my fantasy and actually living it was **action**.

I *did something* and now I live a life others fantasize about. I no longer have to commute on crowded trains and in stand-still traffic. Is the reality as great as the fantasy was?

No. It's better. It can be your reality too.

Ultimately, *The Money Spot*™ *Framework* will enable you to stop dreaming about sending your kids to better schools, take better (and more) holidays and spend more time with family and you can start making that lifestyle a reality.

Enjoy!

PRODUCT

1

You Can Love Your Product Too Much

Loving your product too much is one of the most common reasons a business fails to take off. A great product is not enough for business success. There are fantastic products rotting in warehouses and garages up and down the country simply because their creator loved them too much.

So, what exactly is loving your product too much? When my husband read the title of this chapter he thought that perhaps I had made a typo. I had not.

You see, a good majority of the people who have picked up this book are already passionate about a specific product, their product. They designed it themselves; it is their pride and joy. If you're a craftsperson, all you think about is your next design whether it be a lampshade or the next piece of furniture you will upcycle. It's the nature of being creative and artistic. However, this obsession can come at the exclusion of everything else that is needed to hit *The Money Spot*™.

You need to love your prospective customer, the person you are trying to help, many times more than you love your product. Loving your customer means connecting with them on a regular basis, *creating content* for them: email them, make videos for them, chat with them on social networks, respond to their email enquiries.

This *Product* section should ideally have been placed after *Branding* and *Marketing* because when those two considerations are in place product success should surely follow. However, I had to hit the product-obsessed early. From the outset I want you to realize that a great product is necessary but not sufficient for business success. In fact, a well-branded and well-marketed *mediocre* product will fly off the shelves leaving the *great* product far behind.

If all you have is a product and no sales you don't have a business – yet.

When I launched *The Money Spot*™ Program I received a call from a woman who had created a hair care line. I'll call her Vicky. She had designed it because her daughter reacted badly to all commercial products, so she decided she would try to make something herself. Soon she was making hair care products for her whole family. It dawned on her that this could be a business so she started making products for sale on a small scale. By the time she was calling me she had been trying to build the business for two years with little success.

She loved her products but she had no idea how she could translate that passion into a business. She said she hated her job. All she did at work was read about formulating hair products.

I asked her questions so I could figure out what her strategy was. One key problem for her was that cash was tight. I asked her what her plan was for manufacturing her designs – did she want to do it herself or use a contract manufacturer? She didn't really know what that was, nor how it worked. I asked her what her cost of production was and how many units she wanted to make for her first batch. She hadn't thought about it. I didn't even get to asking her about branding and marketing before she burst into tears.

I was stunned, as I hadn't experienced this before but I was also moved that she felt she could open up to me like that.

When she had pulled herself together, she said she'd reacted that way because she was realizing that she hadn't thought anything through. She had started ordering ingredients to create products for sale without even calculating the per unit cost and she had no strategy for selling products other than a small local salon offering to display them for her.

This is the best example I've seen of someone who is so into their product they can't see beyond it.

TO HIT THE MONEY SPOT™

a great product is necessary but not sufficient. You must love your customer more than the product.

2

If You Must Make Your Own Products, Get A Marketing Enthusiast

Some people can't help themselves – they simply can't find enough hours in the day to work on both their product and their customer. If this is you, then you need to find someone else to work on your branding and marketing on a consistent, daily basis while you work on your product.

Vicky told me she simply had to make her own products because she couldn't trust anyone else to get it right. However, once you've come up with a hair care product the formula is fixed – I know this because I formulate myself, so I asked, 'You think a factory with all the correct machinery and measuring tools is more likely to get your formula wrong than you doing it yourself?'

Vicky said she just felt more comfortable doing it herself. Our phone call was short so I didn't get into discussing her ability to make large volumes when demand grew. To be honest, she was in such a rut on this particular day that she didn't feel she had a chance to make her business her life. I got the sense that she had decided success was a fantasy for her, it wouldn't happen. After our discussion she was much more hopeful.

If, like Vicky, you want or have to make your own products and have no time for branding and marketing, then getting someone else to do it for you is a must.

Some elements of branding can be cheaply created using services like fiverr.com; on fiverr you can get graphics, video intros, voiceovers and other design work completed for $5 to $25, on average.

I have frequently used fiverr and loved the quality of the work received.

At times, I want to see design work from several designers so I use 99designs or DesignCrowd. The two sites work in a similar fashion. You post a job describing exactly what you want. Designers then work on your brief and submit designs. They keep tweaking the designs until you are happy with them. If you don't guarantee a win you can reject all the designs and pay nothing. That said, you will always get more design submissions if you guarantee the project.

Pro Tip

Always make your design contests blind, so that designers can't see each other's work. Creative designers hate submitting to open contests because they don't want to be copied.

When it comes to the marketing elements of your business, you could get a business partner who works on that side of things whilst you focus on the product. If you don't want to partner up with someone then consider getting a part-time, paid employee. This is what I did: –

After 14 months of doing all my own marketing I wanted to double my efforts, so I hired someone using Elance.com. I gave my Marketing Manager all those marketing elements that I had started finding tedious: responding to email, Instagram and Pinterest postings, reaching out to people to feature on NenoNatural.com. You know what surprised me? She did most jobs better than I ever did.

There I was thinking no one could market my business better than I do and within three months Alani was shining. I took the time to train her properly from the start and it paid off. Over time, as my confidence in her grew I gave her more and more tasks; for instance, when my Facebook Inbox became unmanageable she got that too. This allowed me to focus on writing books, blogs and creating videos.

TO HIT THE MONEY SPOT™
marketing efforts have to be consistent. If you don't have the time for marketing, showing your customers love, get someone else to do it.

3

You Don't Have To Make Your Own Products

I almost fell into this trap.

I made the first batch of the first product I designed and by default I thought, *well, to produce more, I need to get a machine.*

I contacted a few bottling companies in China and received their quotes. I liked the look of one of them and decided I was going to go ahead with that purchase so I requested a pro forma invoice and contract so I could pay the deposit.

For some reason, the manufacturer didn't reply immediately. In the meantime, I started getting cold feet: I realized the number of bottles I needed to sell to recoup the cost of the machine was huge. Then I needed to source all the ingredients that went into my product, the bottles, the labels and I needed to manage logistics. It sounded like one big hassle to me.

Then I thought, I spend all day, every day, writing blogs and editing videos – exactly where am I going to find the extra time to manufacture? Also, I only have one product now, how do I plan on expanding into additional products? I can't afford to hire people. Two days later when I got a response from the bottling machine manufacturer I realized I had been moments away from making the biggest mistake of my life. I changed tack.

I decided to focus on the US although I lived in London, because most of my fans were there. I had already been working with a small company in California that had created a custom oil pack for me and decided to check their ability to produce my custom oil blend too. I gave them my formula and they quoted a decent price for making 300 bottles. They sourced all the raw materials including the packaging. I ordered labels online and got them shipped directly to them.

It was so easy.

I created a product listing on Amazon. Once the bottles had been produced, my California supplier shipped them directly to an Amazon fulfillment center for me. It was all hassle free. Now that my California supplier has expanded into label printing that's something else I don't need to order separately; I just send my finished label designs to them.

I would never have enjoyed making my own products. In fact, I would have hated it. I enjoy creative work, I despise admin. Coming up with the product formulation is creative. Once you are happy with your product and your formula is fixed you need to be able to mass produce – anyone can do that for you.

There are a fixed number of hours in a day and the way I see it, you need to spend them where you will add the most value. If you are a creative and your strength is in product design, then design more new products. Build your audience by creating more content – blogs, videos, podcasts. This is where sustained growth will come from.

Don't become a manufacturer by default. Manufacturing is probably not the best use of your time, and your money, and, especially in the early days of building your brand and business, is a precious resource that shouldn't be wasted on machinery.

TO HIT THE MONEY SPOT™
make sure you are consistently using your time, energy and money where the most value lies – in profit-generating tasks. Assign admin and repetitive tasks to others.

4

Bootstrap Your Success Using Other People's Products

When I started running NenoNatural.com as a business, I was running out of cash. I knew I needed to spend money to make money, but I didn't have much to spare.

At the time, I noticed that a lot of the competition were running product giveaways to attract people to their website and endear themselves to their fans – after all, who doesn't like free stuff? I knew to get more attention I ought to do the same, so I decided to contact small hair product companies to give me free products to give away.

I hadn't yet read *The 7 Habits of Highly Effective People* by Stephen Covey yet but intuitively I was thinking win-win (the fourth habit); I knew no one would give me anything for free unless there was something in it for them. I decided to offer each company a free blog post in which they explained the products they were giving away to my audience. At the time I had about 5,000 Facebook fans and 1,000 email subscribers so I called my email *Free Promo to 5,000 fans* or something along those lines.

It was easy to use Facebook, Twitter and Google to find companies that make hair care products. To encourage a response I made their life easy: I told each company that they didn't have to send the products to me. I would run their giveaway for them and introduce their products to my audience. Once the competition was won, I would send them the winners' details so they could send products directly to them. I emphasized that this would also enable them to solicit reviews directly if the winner liked their range.

Most companies didn't bother to reply – perhaps my title was too spammy, but I received enough responses to continue running product giveaways once or twice a month until I had my own range of products to sell and give away.

I could have got more responses by sending follow-up emails and making phone calls but I didn't need to.

My strategy was win-win-win:

My audience won because they had been asking me to introduce them to new products that they didn't know about. In addition, the giveaway winners received free products.

The product companies won because they were getting free marketing.

I won because I was able to build my audience by giving away products without having to buy them.

As my audience grew, I discovered a new way of using other people's products to grow my own authority and audience: product reviews. Attracted by my growing Facebook audience, companies started asking me to review their products. Sometimes I got the products for free, but I made it clear that I would give a fair and honest review regardless. There was no value in lying. Saying a bad product was good would keep the product company happy but alienate my audience – and they mattered a million times more.

Success breeds success. At one point I had so much free product I didn't know what to do with it. I decided to stop doing product reviews because I was by now selling successfully on Amazon and the extra money meant I was in a position to expand in different ways.

Receiving products from newly-established companies provided unexpected lessons in branding. I had subscribed to Glossy Box – a monthly beauty product sample box – then was approached by a new natural hair product box to do a review.

The contrast in quality was stark: the hair product box had very poorly-branded products, some with unreadable labels. There was no write-up explaining each product and brand as Glossy Box has. It was atrocious.

Six months later, the website of the natural hair box was taken down. I assume they couldn't consistently source enough high-quality products, and given the poor quality of their products, subscribers were unsubscribing. Aesthetics do matter.

TO HIT THE MONEY SPOT™
grow your authority using product giveaways and honest product reviews. Learn from the mistakes of competing companies — you don't have to make every mistake yourself!

5

Forget Bootstrapping.
Make Other Brands Your Full-time Business

This is the lowest risk strategy for building a business and lots of people have done it, mostly by growing an audience on YouTube, Instagram or other social network.

Video is the most intimate way to build an audience. People who consistently choose to watch your videos actually like you, your voice and your delivery. This makes a YouTube audience a very dedicated and loyal fan base, compared to fans on other social networks.

If you grow a big enough audience, people will want to have access to it by asking you to review or introduce a product to them.

With a product *review* you tell your audience what you like about the product, what you might like improved and perhaps compare it to similar products that you've used.

With a product *introduction*, you explain how a product is used and how it looks or works on you.

So, how do you build this audience? Create high-quality content on the chosen platform, be it a blog or social media. Use appropriate hashtags so that people find you, post consistently and advertise a little to grow.

There is much more on building an audience in the marketing section so I won't write too much here; for now I wanted to highlight that you can make a good living by marketing other people's products. In some cases you can earn enough just from YouTube's ad revenues so you don't need companies to sponsor you in any way.

TO HIT THE MONEY SPOT™
*build your authority
around a niche so that you
can make a good living off
the ad revenue and
sponsorships — where you
choose to do them.*

6

Be Mindful Of The Biggest Emerging Trend

The internet changed and is still changing the way that business is done, especially how people want to communicate with the brands that they support.

People want to get personal with their brands. They want to purchase from companies and people they relate to. No one wants you to *sell* anything to them, they want you to *appeal* to them. They want insight into who you are and what you stand for. They want to buy from companies that stand for the same things that they do.

This need has led to the growth of the micro-celebrity: ordinary people who wield star power by consistently producing content people like. The best example is the birth of the YouTube celebrity – everyday guys and girls making videos in their living room that are watched by thousands of subscribers. Some YouTube celebrities have more dedicated fans than many TV stars because they feel so accessible.

You can no longer base your business around a generic website which shows great-looking products but says nothing about who you are and what you stand for. This would make you a commodity. It's very hard to sell a commodity – nobody wants to buy them. You need to appeal to prospective customers by building a *brand* and *personality* they can admire. Share pictures and a bit of your history.

Find it hard to share information about yourself? Start with your personal Facebook page. Facebook is a safe and reasonably controlled environment where you choose exactly who can see your content. You can have as few or as many friends as you want. Facebook has become the place where many choose to share snippets of their life to a select group. New platforms are cropping up all the time.

I can't believe that in this day and age I have friends who are not on Facebook. I accept it, but I don't get it. To me, choosing not to use Facebook is like making an extra effort not to be in touch with your friends.

The main reason people give for rejecting Facebook is *I feel like you give too much away* – really, so what? What's so dear about your life that it needs to be so guarded? Importantly, you choose what and how much you share. Although I log on daily, I had the same profile picture since I joined the platform in 2007 until 2014 whereas some people change their picture daily.

The only real reason for not using Facebook is that it becomes an addiction that drives you away from work. I totally agree with that reasoning. Even if you have the best self-control in the world you will always spend a little more time on Facebook than you want to. Set a timer to control time wasting.

Why do I enjoy using the platform so much? Ever the nosey parker, it started off with wanting to know what my friends were up to. I like looking at photos of their weddings, birthdays and other achievements. When I started using it for business I found it an excellent platform for debates and discussions with my fan base.

I have had some of the most engaging discussions with fans using Facebook. I will admit, however, that Facebook is getting less interesting and I now find YouTube and Instagram much more worthwhile.

Using a social media platform on a personal basis makes it easier to move into using it for business. If you don't use the platform at all, the learning curve is huge and it will take you longer to build your fan base than is necessary. Every social network works differently and it's best to stick to the one you enjoy using the most.

Keep in mind that once you share something on the internet, even if it's in a private or closed group, it takes on a life of its own because your friends may choose to use it in a way you hadn't foreseen.

Don't try to use every social network: focus on one and make a good effort on two other platforms. Facebook was my initial focus with Twitter and YouTube as close seconds. After a year and a half I decided to make YouTube my focus with Instagram and Facebook as secondary.

TO HIT THE MONEY SPOT™
accept that you are going to have to share some of your life with your fans and followers. You can choose how much you share but know that the more honest and open you seem, the more people will trust you and your brand. People buy from people, not from companies.

7

Chase Work: Money Will Start Chasing You

You've heard it said time and time again: *do what you love*. It's a cliché now and has begun to lose meaning but it's probably the biggest lesson in building a successful business. As a child my dad always said to me, *Heather, don't chase money, chase work and money will start chasing you*. I love the way he put it.

If you love what you do, you don't have to make an effort. You will have to work on it consistently and at times even when you are tired and need a rest, but if you're enjoying yourself, you will not feel the sacrifice as much.

This is what chasing money looks like: you see cash cows instead of seeing people; you think about how you can make money instead of how you can serve a niche; you fail to see the negative consequences of your actions; you build a brand simply to exploit it and make money out of it, instead of building a brand to appeal to an audience you love and want to serve.

I'm not ashamed to say I love women — I have always felt extremely passionate about the progress of women in society and I celebrate it.

I find it hard to write in generic terms. My book coach told me that I shouldn't assume my audience is of a given type – I agree with this to a certain extent but I personally love to write to and for women. I relate to women's problems and I am empathetic towards their wants and needs – writing to a female audience is effortless for me.

Most people enjoy something. This thing you enjoy is the best place to start when it comes to building a business. No matter how niche your interest seems, there are people out there who enjoy the same thing too. Putting yourself out there by writing and vlogging about your passion is the first step in building your audience.

It doesn't matter if someone else is doing something similar. They are not you. Put your own spin on the topic. The same people who like your competitors may not only like you too, they may prefer you. A successful business only requires a small, dedicated and loyal following; it doesn't require the whole world to be into you.

TO HIT THE MONEY SPOT™
*stop chasing money – seek
to serve a small audience by
sharing what you enjoy
with them – chase work
and money will start
chasing you.*

8

So, Where Should You Start?

If you are still in a regular job, the lowest risk strategy is to follow my three-step blueprint to quitting your day job. The strategy below outlines how I went about leaving full-time employment. If you're already running a business full-time or not in a regular job, then you can skip straight to Step Two of the strategy.

When I decided to quit the proverbial 9-to-5 in 2012, several friends tried to discourage me.

One of them explained that being self-employed is hard because you wake up in the morning and are faced with this whole day ahead of you that you have to fill up with work. She'd quit her job before and struggled to make a living, so she returned to working full-time. Basically, she didn't have a proper plan for self-employment; that's why it didn't work out. However, at least she won't regret having tried.

Several of my friends have been talking about quitting for years but they probably never will get past the talking-about-it stage.

Personally, I have been busy from the day I quit, and I have no problems staying motivated to keep working. Here is the strategy I used to move into lucrative full-time self-employment.

If you sit down and think about this strategy properly and work through the exercises you too can ditch being bossed about and become the boss yourself.

Just to give you a flavor of what being the boss entails:

- Working on what you love daily
- Delegating what you don't love to contractors
- Spending way more time with loved ones
- Going on holiday without having to ask anyone else for permission

Basically, living a full life.

Anyhow, I'll stop showing off and get to the strategy so that you too can get this life sooner rather than later. If you build your business the way I have mine, you can run it from anywhere even if you sell physical products. Don't worry, you'll learn all about how to do this under *Distribution*.

Step 1: Plan When

I first became serious about leaving banking and starting my own business in 2009. I wasn't in a position to resign right away, so I set early 2012 as my quitting year.

Before I resigned I needed to buy a family-sized property and I wanted to save a lot more. I calculated that it would take three years to achieve these things. Three years wasn't a random estimate; I listed everything I needed to do, the amount of money I needed to save plus how much I could realistically save per month and three years was the result of using this approach.

At the time, it seemed like a long time, but three years flew by because I threw myself into ticking off everything on the before-I-quit to-do list leaving little time for boredom.

You need to list everything you want to achieve before you can quit work. Importantly, don't put unrealistic or unachievable things on your list or you'll never be in a position to leave.

I have a friend who also wants to buy a home before she starts a business but she can't afford her ideal neighborhood. I told her that no-one starts off living in their ideal neighborhood; you just have to buy where you can afford. Frankly, I wanted to live in a more upmarket neighborhood myself, but I decided that the people in my home (great husband and any kids to come) are far more important than my address.

I chose a neighborhood where I could afford a bigger house and I wasn't willing to compromise on size simply to live 10 minutes up the road. A house would cost two to three times more in my ideal neighborhood. If I had decided to save towards living there I would still be miserably working in investment banking.

OK, I think you get the point, let's start with your Step 1 exercise. Get a piece of paper to write down your answers.

EXERCISE – Planning When to Quit

What do you need to get done before you can quit your day job?

E.g. get married, build a website, write a book, develop a product, develop an online social following or an email list, get a business loan or personal loan, get some business coaching etc

What is the minimum amount of income you can live on per month?

In the first days of running a business you will need to be frugal. So, don't write the income you need to live the ideal life, we're talking bare minimums here. E.g. before I quit I made sure to secure an interest-only mortgage. This reduced the mortgage payments, our biggest monthly expense, by about 50%.

How much will it cost to run your business per month?

You will need a budget for commissioning art work, maintaining an email list, ordering initial stocks of product, paying for software and so on. It cost about £600-£1,000 ($1,000-$1,500) per month to run my business in the early days.

How many months will it take for you to save 12 months' worth of personal and business expenses?

This will be the sum of what you worked out in the two previous questions multiplied by 12. If you have partner who can support your business, then this amount doesn't need to be so large. You should still save something for personal needs, gifts, and running the business.

How long will it realistically take to achieve the above goals – financial and business/product development?

You now know when you will quit.

Get a piece of paper or post-it note, write the month and year on it and stick it in a place where you will see it every day.

To help produce a realistic timeline:

* Find out what it realistically costs to run a business monthly when you start up. A business coach or experienced friend can help with this exercise

* Get reliable quotes on how much your product will cost to make

Step 2: Plan What

Before you quit, you need to decide exactly what sort of business you want to be running. I now own a hair care business but my initial plan was to coach people on how to get into investment banking. To be honest, I settled on the coaching idea simply because it was what I knew best, not what I would enjoy working on the most.

It wasn't nearly as fun as running my hair care business. I would advise you to think through the business you want to run very carefully and more strategically than I did.

EXERCISE – Planning What To Do When You Quit

What do you enjoy doing the most in your spare time?

E.g. sewing, makeup, styling your hair, researching skin products, knitting, upcycling furniture, shopping (this can be a career if you're a good shopper, e.g. if you're an expert at finding bargains or you have a sense of style that would appeal to many), making jewelry, etc

Do you need to take any courses on what you want to do or can you just research online as you go along?

For my hair blog I learned as I went along. I looked for scientific research to inform my blogs and the hair routines I developed. I did take courses on how to make hair care products later but this was not a prerequisite to quitting my job. You can do the same.

How will you make an income from this niche? That is, what products would you like to develop or promote?

By the time you release products you will already have a significant following grown while you had a job, so it will be a less risky proposition.

You don't have to sell physical products; you can provide information products only – the start-up cost will be much lower but it's not zero. Even maintaining a large email list costs money.

If you want to develop authority on a physical product, remember that you don't have to sell physical products you make yourself. You can sell third-party products, or earn money solely from advertising. If you execute the Marketing section of *The Money Spot*™ framework to perfection, you might be able to make a full six-figure living from advertising.

OK, so the business you will grow is decided.

Step 3: Get As Much In Place As You Can

You now know exactly how much money you need before you can quit and you have figured out how long it will take to get that together. That was Step 1.

In Step 2, you decided what business you would be venturing into and how you plan to make an income out of it.

Now, you need to write a weekly schedule of things that you will do until you quit your job. If your day job is in the type of industry that requires your personal ventures to operate under a pseudonym that is fine – you can have a unique logo and pseudonym. I would still strongly recommend using YouTube for growth; the likelihood of clients from your day job stumbling upon you is low so don't be worried about being found.

Investment banks typically don't want their staff to have businesses on the side or online profiles not related to their job so having videos on YouTube was a little risky while I was working there, but I did it anyway. I just didn't use my real name.

EXERCISE – Working Your Pre-Quit Plan

List everything you want to have completed by the time you quit – in specific terms

E.g. number of blogs and vlogs per week; words per blog; build website; develop products x, y and z; get all brand elements in place; write report, blueprint or book on x.

Organize your goals into monthly and weekly objectives using the free Objectives Template at katsonga.com/resources

You will have to spend two to four hours on your business every day to achieve your objective of quitting your job. Some nights I was tired after work, but I did a little something anyway. I was working on a book at the time and 30 minutes of writing was better than nothing at all.

If you don't know how to implement some of the things you want to achieve then get a coach or join a program that will take you through them.

That's it. You have everything you need to start.

TO HIT THE MONEY SPOT™
you don't need a detailed business plan before you start. Get a piece of paper and mind map your strategy using the steps above. Most of the strategies above can be applied regardless of your current employment status.

BRANDING

1

Everyone Judges Books By Their Cover

People make an instant judgement on what they see.

I started thinking about this most critically after I self-published my first book, *To Become an Investment Banker: Girl Banker®'s Bullet Point Guide to Highflying Success*. A guy from Argentina (of all places) wrote to me saying, essentially, *I loved your book but the cover is horrible.*

I was hurt, but I contacted a few book cover designers to ask them what they thought. Based on feedback the cover was immediately changed and, lo and behold, sales started to rise immediately.

To prove this critical point further, when I was invited to talk in schools I took both versions of the book, with the old and the new cover, to see which people preferred. I still expected them not to care, especially when I told them the content was identical, but everyone wanted the book with the new cover.

The lesson which I carried into all future businesses was clear:

TO HIT THE MONEY SPOT™

pay very careful attention to aesthetics — people judge the look of a product in seconds and that first impression will impact whether or not they decide to explore the product further.

2

Choose Your Tone

I have always had a preference for a more laid back, conversational tone. I wrote that way in my university essays and I wrote that way to clients at work. Luckily it's the perfect tone for beauty businesses and women-focused businesses in general.

First things first, what do I mean by a tone?

Your tone is the way that you sound to your readers. It should vary according to your audience. There are a wide variety of tones to choose from:

* Formal
* Serious
* Casual without being over-familiar
* Conversational
* Flamboyant and arty
* Curt or brief
* Long-winded
* Funny

To pick the ideal tone you need to consider who you are speaking to rather than writing the way you speak by default; your style has to reflect the audience. Ask yourself the following:

Who are you writing for?
* Men, women, or children?
* Young or old?
* Well-educated or less educated?
* Religious or not religious?
* Employed or self-employed?
* White collar or blue collar?
* What's their political stance – liberal or conservative?

Different groups of people expect a certain tone and can be very put off if you pick the wrong one. For instance, 99% of my fans are black and of these 80% are women. If I made an anti-Obama post I would be very likely to get a lot of people unliking my page. Black people in America are for the most part Democrat; Republican or right-wing statements will not win me any favors.

Fortunately, I am very liberal myself. That said, I try to stay away from politics unless I can't help myself.

What is the personality of your readers?

Are they more formal or casual? A blog targeted at well-off, professional working mothers requires a different tone (and even content) to one targeting low-income stay-at-home mothers, the so called homemakers – I love that word.

One group may prefer a straightforward, no nonsense tone; the other may want a little more creativity and sensitivity.

Finally, what is the goal of your reader?

The reason people choose to watch you on YouTube or read your blogs should inform your tone. It could be:

* Beauty
* Education
* Fitness
* Fun and entertainment
* Guidance
* Relaxation

For instance, my earlier YouTube videos were far too formal and educational and that may be why growth was slow to start. Once I infused a lot more fun into them and became much more casual, views went up and the comments reflected higher engagement from people watching.

Comments such as 'I can really see the fun side of you in that video' let me know I was on the right track. Frankly, it took me a long time to realize my tone could be different.

TO HIT THE MONEY SPOT™
pick a tone that will engage your audience from the start. To do this figure out who you are speaking to, what their personality is and what they want from you or your business.

3

Don't Be Color Blind

Especially for beauty products, the colors you use will influence customer decisions. However, this is not limited to the color on packaging. You need to think strategically about the colors you use for marketing.

You have to use a color scheme that will appeal to your specific audience. Most of us decide on brand colors depending on our own taste and style. Taste and style are fine but they have to be subservient to the goal of influencing a decision.

For instance, I have loved green forever. There are many things green is good for but payment buttons is not usually one of them. I was about to make the awful decision of having payment buttons in green when I learned that red and orange buttons have higher conversion rates. Say what? Yes, apparently, it's so.

Here are some guidelines for picking color:

Emphasize what you want the customer to look at

When you use colors you also need to emphasize the right objects. If you get a developer to build your website be completely mindful that their expertise is not in marketing but in technology. They need you to tell them what to do to create a look that will influence decisions.

For instance, my coaching program has three main packages and I knew that to help the customer I needed to highlight the most popular one. What my developer came back with was a website that highlighted the two packages that I didn't want highlighted. As far as he was concerned he had technically done the job right. As far as I was concerned it was a bad job because his work did nothing to help the customer decide. If anything, the customer would be even more confused.

When you go to savvy e-commerce sites you will notice that 'pay' buttons are bright and stand out easily, and 'cancel transaction' buttons are grey so that you don't focus on them.

Overall, when you look at any work involving color on your website, product or corporate stationery think:

* Am I emphasizing what I want the customer to look at?
* Will it influence their decision positively?

If you answer 'yes' to both, you have done a good job.

Use the right combination of colors

Some color combinations look wacky or simply tacky. It doesn't necessarily mean that those colors can't be used together but perhaps that they should be used in different amounts. If you have two very strong colors then perhaps one should be dominant and the other used less.

If you have a dark background then in order to stand out text needs to be white. You should always make text easy for the customer to read.

Use color to portray your message

Say your ideal customer is a wealthy professional mother who lives in a sophisticated neighborhood. She is a senior VP at a blue chip company. In her spare time she plays golf at a country club. She holidays in the Hamptons and skis in France during the winter. She has a husband and two teenage kids.

Whatever products you create need to say, *I am quality, I am expensive, I am worth being seen with your Ralph Lauren gym bag.*

Now say your ideal customer is her daughter instead. She is very fun loving; likes to party. She is the cool girl at school; her peers emulate her and she likes this attention. She knows and loves all the latest music. She is beautiful as well as fit.

Whatever products you create need to say, *I am young, I am cool, I have great taste, buy me to proliferate your cool chick image.*

These two customers will probably buy similar-priced products but they want to achieve completely different aims. The daughter's products are likely to be more colorful and the mother's more understated.

If you looked at the mother's dresser vs. the daughter's dresser you'd probably see a completely different feel of products.

The father and son too will be attracted to totally different things. They have different social goals and purchase products that fulfill those goals.

TO HIT THE MONEY SPOT™

use color to attract and influence your ideal customer. Don't allow your own taste and style to overpower the need to influence a favorable decision by your target customer.

4

Have A Logo That Means Something

Logos are a crucial brand identifier.

I believe one of the reasons that the number of Neno Natural fans on Facebook grew so rapidly from day one is because I have an attractive logo that clearly depicts me and my fans' interest: kinky and curly hair. The logo is a tasteful black and white and cost a mere $25.

You don't have to spend a huge amount on logo design. In fact, some of the biggest brands spent negligible amounts having their now widely-recognized logos created: Twitter paid $15 and Nike $35 (inc.com).

You should invest your time and energy on thinking about what you want your logo to say about your brand and whether it will work on all the different platforms you want to use it.

Before we talk about your logo, I'll explain how my logo was born.

My Logo's Story –
NenoNatural.com, Kinky & Curly Hair Blog

The logo people see at NenoNatural.com was not even designed for that business. It was designed for my investment banking coaching business, girlbanker.com. However, the logo, with a minor adjustment, was adapted for NenoNatural.com easily

At the time I was having the girlbanker.com logo designed I was going through a difficult time at work because I had changed my hair from being straight to an afro texture. It caused quite a stir on the trading floor and people asked me the most absurd questions. The artistic afro look is definitely not the look investment banks want to portray but I didn't care. I wanted my hair to look closer to the way it grows rather than have society dictate that I use straightening products.

When I sat down to mind map my logo, I wanted my logo to say:

cool, classy, timeless, upmarket

Then I wanted it to reflect *me;* the major thing going on in my life at that time was that I had natural, afro-textured hair, so the logo portrayed that.

This is the original logo:

My logo has very important features that matter to me.

The afro, as explained above.

The direction. The face is looking forwards for a reason; I was near paranoid about not having a face that looks backwards – I like to look forwards, towards the future, because that's where hope lies.

The hoop-earring and distinctive eyelash. These two elements say I'm cool and fashionable.

Black and white says timeless, classy and upmarket.

The **currency symbols** bring finance into it. Their order is from the most traded to least traded hard currency.

To adapt the logo for NenoNatural.com I just removed the currency symbols and it worked:

Ultimately, it turned out that I designed a very flexible logo that could be adapted for many different functions. When I wanted a silhouette designed for my Queen of Kinks, Curls & Coils® hair care brand, the logo plopped itself very neatly on the head of my silhouette:

The silhouette sometimes has green elements added to reflect harmony with nature; NenoNatural.com is about being as natural and authentic as possible.

Developing Your Logo

You don't have to go through an identical process to design your logo. It doesn't have to portray you, the person, but it does have to represent your brand and your business.

There are many different types of logos out there. For some the name of the company is the logo, think eBay and Google, yet others use just a symbol, think the Nike swoosh or Apple's apple.

You should also use colors to evoke specific emotions or to reflect the brand's purpose. Do not use colors simply because they are your favorite, without consideration of what the colors actually mean to people.

Before you go out to find a logo designer, either through 99designs.com or a branding company, have a huge brainstorm regarding:
* what the logo should represent;
* which colors you will use and why;
* how it will reflect your business' values and slogans;
* what products you might want to attach it to and so on.

Draw a mind map with lots of different lines describing everything you want your logo to capture.

If you start the design process without a clear concept you will end up with a logo that doesn't speak to your desired following.

If you use an effective symbol to represent your brand, people will think of your brand even when all other brand elements are missing. A study by the University of Amsterdam used famous symbol-based logos without wording (such the Nike swoosh/tick) to figure out when children start to recognize brands. Two hundred and thirty four Amsterdam-based children were surveyed.

By age three to five, children start to recognize that a logo represents a certain product and when they are seven or eight, they can consistently recognize the logo and the brand it represents. So, you'll show them the Nike tick and they will say 'Nike shoes' or something similar immediately. This is good branding. Why would any 10-year-old be pleased with no-name pair of sneakers for Christmas when by that age they already know and recognize Nike as a premium, well-known brand.

In the long-run, your $50-200 logo could be worth millions on its own. Nike's $35 tick symbol is worth billions.

TO HIT THE MONEY SPOT™

get a good quality, well-designed logo that evokes the specific emotions you want it to.

5

What's Your Slogan?

Yes, you need one of these too. Something simple and memorable.

Think, Nike's *Just do it.*

A slogan doesn't have to cost anything at all – you can sit down and think of it yourself. Supermarkets are fantastic with slogan usage. I shop at Sainsbury's supermarket and every few minutes the speaker system blares, *Sainsbury's, Live Well For Less* and each and every time I find myself speaking along. The slogan is said by exactly the same female voiceover in every store. The consistency helps to strengthen the brand.

Budget chain supermarket Iceland always finishes its TV ads with *That's why mums go to Iceland*, followed by a clinking of coins to represent money saved. Now that I'm pregnant I recognize just how incredibly powerful the word 'mum' is in that slogan. Personally, I don't shop there but nonetheless, I know and recognize their branding well.

This is exactly what you want. You want your branding to nurture prospects.

Everyone exposed to your brand who is not a customer is a prospect. There may come a time when they need something and as a result of your branding they choose to come to you.

Your slogan should summarize what a prospect gets; it should fulfill a need. So, in my mind, for example, *Just do it* brings to mind someone who wants to get fit and perhaps doesn't feel motivated but they think, I'll *just do it* like Nike says I should. Or perhaps they feel fully motivated but are doubting whether they have trained enough to win a race and they think, I'll *just do it* and see what happens. *Just do it* will mean different things to different people but it fully captures the essence of action and motion – exactly what a sports brand would want.

There are some slogans that most people know. For instance:
* I'm lovin' it
* Finger lickin' good

If you don't know which brands use the above slogans, I'm slightly worried.

How can you come up with your own killer slogan? What rules do you need to follow?

These are my seven rules for coming up with a slogan:

- Keep it simple.
- Don't use foreign words or little known words
- Your slogan comes after the logo creation. It needs to capture everything your logo does but now as a phrase rather than a name or symbol. Use the same mind map you created for your logo to start coming up with possible slogans. Think from the perspective of your customer's problem not according to your own wants, needs and tastes
- Be funny without being obscure
- If you use a play on words make it something your niche will actually understand. Don't try to be too clever
- The slogan should fully capture what your product or brand actually does. 'Just do it' and 'I'm lovin' it' are pretty obscure, in fact, but they have been so well-promoted so consistently and so persistently over such a prolonged period of time that everyone does know them. 'Finger lickin' good' is not obscure – it says our chicken is so good you'll lick your fingers and is completely fitting for a fried chicken chain
- Finally, if you can't come up with something good yourself or don't have a team to brainstorm with, hire someone to help

TO HIT THE MONEY SPOT™
come up with a killer slogan that captures the exact problem your prospective customers want to solve.

6

Don't Commit To One Designer

Unless you're an artist you're going to need graphics work done for you: headers for your website and social networks, eBook covers, product labels, brochures, leaflets, thumbnails for videos and infographics for your website.

Even if you can do great design work yourself, sometimes you don't have the time or need someone with a slightly different skill or perspective to yours.

This is what I've learned when it comes to designers: **don't assume a local designer will be better than someone you find on the internet.** Working with a recommended designer can lead to a pressure you don't need and reduces your flexibility and choices. Okay, I feel like I'm speaking in tongues so I'll just come out and say what I mean.

One of my contract manufacturers suggested a designer that they thought would be *perfect* for me. When I asked to see her portfolio it did indeed look amazing. As she was based in the UK I knew she would be charging a premium relative to most other designers because the British cost of living is high, but I was willing to pay for top notch work.

Luckily, I had the chance to test her out before committing the design of my product labels to her. I wanted one of my logos changed so I gave her the job with a detailed brief of likes, dislikes, dos and don'ts.

The first thing that annoyed me is that she needed two weeks just to show me her first draft and when I got it I couldn't quite believe it was her work. It looked like she had gotten some kid to do it. Her re-work took another two weeks and what she came back with was exactly what I had asked for with no real creative input from her; she hadn't built on my vision. The best graphic designers I have worked with always surprised me by improving on my ideas or suggesting something I had not thought of.

I would have liked to see more variations on the logo but she was charging per hour so I didn't push it. I already felt like I was being overcharged given the shoddy designs that I had seen thus far.

When I got the final files the .png images didn't have a transparent background as they should – that is amateur – and some of the images were so low res they weren't even good enough for the internet. I had to ask for better quality images.

Her portfolio suggested she was a good designer but I learned quickly that being emotionally invested in your designer makes it harder. I did give her critical feedback after receiving the atrocious first draft and I felt guilty about that.

After that I decided crowd design sites such as 99designs.com were the best solution for me. They work well because the price is fixed so once you choose your package you don't need to worry about money; the timeline is fixed, seven days from the start to the end of the project and frequently faster if you choose to award a winner early; you're not emotionally or personally connected to the designer so you don't feel guilty for asking to see different variations – if the designer gets tired of you they can just opt out of the competition; best of all you see the artistic input of several designers before committing to one – on my best projects I had over 70 submissions from a handful of designers.

DesignCrowd and CrowdSpring are other popular options. I haven't tried CrowdSpring but I have used DesignCrowd, it's OK but I prefer 99designs' interface. Google 'crowd design site' to find other options.

If you're on a tight budget fiverr.com is a good place to start. I have found good designers on there but sometimes it's hit and miss.

TO HIT THE MONEY SPOT™

use great quality graphics from qualified designers. Use crowd design sites for great, customer-grabbing graphics.

7

Don't Skimp On Packaging

Perception is reality.

I love that phrase. The truth is what everyone *else* thinks it is; what you think pretty much doesn't matter.

Think of yourself as a product and your friends as your customers. Do they see you as introverted or extroverted?

Almost everyone thinks I am an extrovert. So, as far as most are concerned, *that is what I am* and they expect my behavior to conform to that: be loud, outgoing and gregarious.

However, if you define extroversion as drawing energy from crowds and introversion as having energy taken away from you by too much exposure to people then I have many introverted characteristics. Do my thoughts matter? Not really – but it does mean people sometimes get offended because they don't understand that I often can't stand crowds. I'm a mixture of extrovert and introvert, but only my closest friends know that.

Sometimes I want peace and quiet so much that any noise will unsettle me, I like to get away. Someone will ask, *what's wrong, you're so quiet?* There is not usually anything wrong, I may just be enjoying a personal thought.

Your products will be judged based on how they are initially perceived.

If you create the wrong first impression you won't attract your ideal customer. If you create a good enough first impression to get a purchase, make sure you live up to it.

Designing Your Packages

Colors, size, shapes and fonts will either appeal or repel your customer in seconds.

Kids prefer lively, engaging colors; artistic people appreciate quirky fonts and shapes; a more conservative professional will be attracted to a sober, understated look.

Your branding gives signals of quality or lack thereof. Frequently, small, cottage-industry brands sell products at markets with illegible fonts, printing that rubs off easily and very cheap packaging. You would never see this quality of product in a reputable store. The message there is that it's a gone-tomorrow brand. It's going to be hard work to market a product that doesn't look like it's going anywhere but the bin.

Premium or Budget

Price is usually used to indicate whether a brand is priced for *affordability* or *status/quality*. Premium products will tend to use higher quality ingredients or will be made better.

Numerous studies involving a variety of products from wine to medicine have found that people judge higher-priced products as better even when exactly the same product is inside the package. Go figure.

Those who buy high-quality goods aren't necessarily doing so to show off. In many instances they have just reached a certain stage when they can afford to buy better quality items. Many of the premium products they buy never leave their home; only their closest friends see them.

For instance, at one friend's house all products may be supermarket value brands; whilst at another friend's house everything is niche and high-status. If you had just created a premium product you'd probably have better luck marketing it to the latter. Perception of product price is totally different on a salary of $2,000/month compared to $20,000/month.

Ultimately, when you package a product you have to think about who you want to buy it and what they should be thinking if and when they choose to purchase. If you try to appeal to everyone you will appeal to no one.

TO HIT THE MONEY SPOT™

package your products exactly as you want them to be perceived by your ideal customer.

8

Face For Radio? Get It Out There Anyway

I recommend that you get vlogging or creating business-related videos as soon as possible.

Most people would never upload a video of themselves to YouTube because they lack the confidence to do so. They will come up with all sorts of excuses including 'my business isn't that type of business,' but the truth is that they simply don't feel comfortable or confident enough. So, I'm going to launch into all the ways you can tackle this issue.

First and foremost note that I did struggle with doubt myself and I'm sure even the massively overconfident Donald Trump thought about what sort of a response he would get for his random YouTube videos that often have nothing to do with the title.

This is my 19-part plan for tackling stage fright:

1 Don't over-think it

It's just a video. Excuses like 'I'm a personal person', 'I'm a private person' and 'I don't want to be on the internet' are too vague.

Firstly, you never ever have to reveal private information about yourself; you can stick to your product or business. Secondly, you will never meet the vast majority of people who will watch your videos but you will build a relationship with them anyway.

And, why the need for such extreme privacy? What's so scary about sharing a little about wonderful you?

Don't over analyze what making videos means.

2 Focus on the product

Stop thinking about yourself and focus entirely on the product or your business. You will feel more comfortable to record when you think in this way.

3 Do relaxation exercises

Meditate or breathe to relax. Google 'relaxation exercises' or 'relaxation techniques' and see what you find.

4 Visualize

Visualization has been scientifically shown to improve performance in elite athletes and other top performers. Visualize making a great recording, editing it successfully and your audience loving it. Visualize as often as possible to build your confidence: try, first thing in the morning and just before bed.

5 Address your real fears one by one

I'm not pretty enough? Nobody's perfect. Accept any flaws that you think you have. Even the people you think have a perfect face or body, think they don't – that's just how life works.

I'm too fat? Accept you're plus-sized or start working out. Exercise should make you feel better even before you lose any weight.

No one will watch? Well then you have nothing to lack confidence about, do you? Get recording. You will see how slowly my viewing numbers rose in the section on marketing. Did I care? Not at all. I celebrated getting 1,000 channel views because I had never expected anyone to watch my videos in the first place. I wasn't comparing myself to those with thousands of subscribers and millions of channel views. Everyone starts with zero.

I feel stupid recording myself? So, what? Just record anyway. Everyone feels stupid at some point. They just choose not to focus on that.

People who know me will laugh *at* me or think poorly of me? Does it matter? What have they done? It is very likely that the people you care about aren't even real friends so investing time in worrying about their response is a waste of your time.

I have a disability? People are very open-minded nowadays. Most of us can look beyond whatever disability you have. Importantly, you will inspire other people, both those with a disability and those without one, to take action. Personally, I am more inspired by someone that has to cope with a disability because I'm like, *if she can do it, what excuse do I really have.*

6 Wear makeup

Makeup is the perfect mask. I always wear too much makeup. I say, if people are going to take the time to watch my videos then I'll take the time to look pretty for them.

You don't even have to do your makeup differently every time. I have been doing it the same way for two years straight with only slight variations, and very few have complained about that.

7 Practise with an audience of one

Practice builds confidence. You may feel a little awkward even with one person watching you, but that builds your confidence anyway.

8 Practise on your own

Sometimes I felt so uncomfortable with my audience of one, my husband, that he had to go away. I could only record in front of myself. This was OK because I knew if I didn't like the recording I could delete it and no one would see it anyway.

9 Prepare material in advance and practise

Practising what you will record will make you feel more comfortable about doing it. Over time you'll find yourself not having to practice before you start recording.

10 Quit trying to be perfect

Nobody is and you're no exception. Sorry to break that to you. Accept that you might hate something about most videos you eventually upload to the internet and that it's OK. Perfection is not what wins fans and breeds loyalty.

11 Convince yourself that your content is the bee's knees

Realize the value of your content. Believe that the work you are doing and the content you are producing is the best ever and *your niche* will absolutely love it.

It's better to nurture 1,000 loyal fans that you would have never met by uploading video content than to miss making an impact on those people completely by keeping all your knowledge to yourself. My personal goal is 100,000 YouTube subscribers. It is an ambitious goal given I am at about 15,000 but it is very achievable.

12 Use screen capture equipment

Instead of recording yourself, record presentation slides as you explain something. I don't recommend doing only this for a beauty business because it is obviously much more impersonal.

Screen capture is much more effective for business tutorials and tutorials on how-to use various software. It is not effective for showing how to paint a bed, sew a cushion or do your makeup.

13 Don't speak to camera

This is one of the biggest confidence boosters. Speaking to camera is very hard. The next best alternative is to record yourself doing something without explaining it. This way you focus on what you are doing without all the nerves regarding what you have to say too.

Then load your video into editing software (e.g. Final Cut Pro, Adobe Premiere Elements etc), mute your recording and speak into the voice recorder to explain what it is you're doing. Most beauty activities are about doing something: your hair, your makeup, other fashion routines, making crafts and so on therefore you can definitely implement this strategy.

14 Record others or events

If you simply can't or rather won't record yourself, then record things related to your product or your business: interview others and record events.

15 Don't try to do it all in one take

Record many clips. If you make a mistake, stop recording and start from the last sentence. Editing is a lot easier when you have lots of clips. It is harder when you have one huge recording to edit.

16 Commit to making video

Decide now that you will continue to upload at least a video a week even if the response in the initial months is slow. Eventually, you will discover which type of videos your niche prefer.

17 Record with no intention to upload

For 14 days straight, record different videos and watch them back a couple of times without the intention of ever putting them onto the internet. The point of the exercise is to practise and therefore improve; in addition, you will realize that you're not as bad as you thought you would be; in fact, you're pretty darn amazing.

18 Create a video character

Instead of recording yourself as the person you think you are, record yourself as the person you want to be. This is as authentic as you can ever be. If you see yourself as Beyoncé then when you're recording your video, imagine that you are her.

If you don't want to be anyone in particular then mind map all the traits you aim to portray and try to reflect them on screen.

19 For heaven's sake, just do it!

Realize that many people upload videos to the internet even though they feel all sorts of negative feelings about it. They just do it.

This chapter is especially detailed because I believe video is such a powerful medium and its importance is growing each and every day. You really can't afford to ignore it.

TO HIT THE MONEY SPOT™
get your face on camera and build relationships with people across the globe. Share your videos on as many social networking platforms as possible.

9

Reveal Your Voice

If no amount of coaxing will get you to make videos, how about getting your voice out instead? Some people have a voice that is so interesting to listen to that they build great relationships with an audience using just that.

I don't podcast very much myself but I would definitely like to do a bit more. Given the limited time I have, I prefer to work on videos. Here are nine good reasons for getting your voice out there:

1 Website traffic

A podcast can bring lots of traffic to your website. Then you have the chance to add people to your email list and showcase your products to them.

2 It's less scary than video

You are revealing just one element of your character, your voice. You don't have to think about how people will judge your clothes, makeup or weight.

3 It's quick and easy

Podcasting is just as easy to do as video – if not easier. You don't have to beautify yourself in any way or think about lighting and camera angles so it's less of a drain on time.

4 Little equipment is involved

All you need is a good microphone; indeed, the microphone that comes with your computer may be good enough. Audacity is free audio-editing software; the only item you would have to invest in is a podcast host (e.g. AudioAcrobat, LibSyn etc).

5 It's another way to build relationships

You build relationships with audio in very much the same way you do with video. If people like what you have to say, enjoy the way that you say it and generally find you entertaining, they will like you as a personality and brand. This relationship may lead to product purchases.

6 You tap into a wider audience

Some people who are interested in your product do not watch YouTube videos at all –they may not have the time. They may not have time to read your blogs. The beauty of audio is that they can consume your content whilst they do something else such as drive. For instance, I prefer to listen to business books in the gym and on my daily walks. I can't walk and watch video, I can't walk and read but I can walk and listen.

This flexibility is probably the biggest difference between the audio platform and video or text-based media.

7 You will get more opportunities

Podcasting is just another way for people to discover you. You can't generate any interest in your products without them (or you) first being discovered. Once you *are* discovered, the possibilities are endless.

Audio does have its limitations. Some tutorials can only be on video because people need to watch how something is done. You can't teach someone how to re-cloth a shoe with an audio tutorial; they need to see you doing it.

Finally, if you do choose to podcast then be consistent. Upload podcasts as often as you commit to doing so.

TO HIT THE MONEY SPOT™

reveal your brand and personality through your voice by podcasting. This is especially important if you're struggling with video. Share links to your podcasts on other social networking platforms.

10

Let Your Fans Smell You!

I first started thinking of multi-sensory branding after reading Roger Dooley's neuromarketing business book, *Brainfluence*.

Did you know that smell is the most sensitive of all our senses, with the strongest link to recalling emotions? There are probably times when a familiar smell from your past evokes strong memories of a certain time and place or reminds you of a specific person.

Neuromarketing studies have found that 75% of emotions are triggered by smell. In addition, studies by the Sense of Smell Institute (yes, such an institution exists) indicate that our recollection of visual images falls to 50% after just three months, but after a whole year we can recall smells with 65% accuracy.

In another study, this time by the Rockefeller University, it was found that in the short-term we remember 1% of what we touch, 2% of what we hear, 5% of what we see, 15% of what we taste and 35% of what we smell!

What does all this mean for your business?

That you need to tap into the power of smell. Businesses tend to focus much more on visuals but in reality sounds and smell can be more effective for branding. Indeed, a visual image is enhanced by associating it with either a brand sound or a brand smell.

According to Pamela Dalton, an olfactory scientist, the sense of smell is well-developed before birth. Studies have found that babies prefer fragrances their mother wore in late pregnancy. This effectively means that we are pre-primed to prefer certain smells. If you're a perfume brand, get expectant mothers on-board to groom your next generation of customers well before they are ready to buy.

How can you expose customers to your brand smell?

Product Scents

If you produce anything that comes in a bottle, choose your scent carefully. Test it on other people to see what they think. Before production of my hair care line, *Queen of Kinks, Curls & Coils*®, I applied the moisturizer on my hair and the first thing my husband and sister-in-law said when they saw me was *'What is that smell, it's amazing!'* That confirmed I had chosen a winning scent for the brand. This is exactly the response you are going for.

Scent Diffusers

You can add a concentrated scent to a diffuser and have it dispersed across a room. Diffusers don't cost much so if you have a shop or book a meeting room you can just take your diffuser along with you.

Large businesses use more sophisticated scent diffusing systems, such as ones that can work with the air conditioning system to diffuse a smell. Some savvy sales people even go to the extent of burning a specific candle in a meeting room for a while before a customer arrives.

Scent Strips

If you send packages with your product, you can get scent strips made that infuse the product with your brand scent. This will especially work for material-based products, e.g. linen, cushions, clothing and other fabric-based products.

Who's Already Using Scent?

The most widely quoted case study is probably that of Singapore Airlines. It was recounted in both *Brainfluence* by Roger Dooley and *Brands & Branding* by Rita Clifton, and it's widely discussed online.

Singapore airlines had a custom aroma formulated called Stefan Floridian Waters which they infuse into many elements of their brand: flight attendants' perfume, the hot towels onboard and throughout each plane.

If you are on a Singapore Airlines flight for even a few hours you become accustomed to the smell, and if you're having great service you come to associate the smell with great service. Exposure to the scent any time after that would result in your recalling the pleasantness of the flight.

Quite a few small and large brands have now started using scent to appeal to their customers. Once you decide on a smell it is not difficult to figure out how to use it more widely to enhance your brand.

TO HIT THE MONEY SPOT™
*build a stronger
relationship with customers
by appealing to their sense
of smell; it is more powerful
than any other sense.*

11

Can They Feel Your Love?

So far the brand elements I have talked about are easily actionable. You can get a better logo, use better colors and improve graphics to maximize aesthetic appeal. You can also come up with a catchy theme song or jingle either on your own or with help from a third-party. And of course, any lab can create a scent for you, should you need one.

This stuff is very much in your control; however, there is really only one thing you want from a fan: a little piece of their heart. You want them to relate to you and your brand and to have genuine affection for you.

A loyal following makes running a business very worthwhile. Without it, it's just meaningless work. You might as well stay in a day job.

A strong relationship with customers leads to brand loyalty, and brand loyalty leads to above average customer retention rates and amazing sales.

According to *Brands & Branding* by Rita Clifton, the strength of the relationship people have with your brand will determine how much they are willing to spend on your products, how long they remain loyal and their willingness to recommend you to their friends and colleagues.

The strength of your relationship improves if customers feel that

* You deliver on promises
* You respect them
* You're open and honest with them
* They have a long-term emotional attachment to you or your brand

and

* They feel that your values are aligned with theirs and there is mutual respect

A degree of consistency builds trust and loyalty.

I'll give a simple example. I decided I would use my Facebook page as a chat and share space and keep promotional stuff to a bare minimum and from the start, I consistently had people writing to say 'I love this page.' They came to know what to expect and to see me as a friend. I too saw them as friends from the start. I wanted coming to my Facebook page to feel like meeting friends at a cafe.

One of my friends used a different strategy: he posted a couple of links to his eBay products daily and he was failing to get any kind of meaningful engagement. He didn't enjoy spending time on Facebook to chat and share things for fun.

Who do you think had a stronger and more meaningful relationship with their fan page?

To my friend, any marketing efforts that didn't involve trying to sell something were a waste of time; this kind of thinking is completely incorrect. People don't only buy things because you've put them in front of them at that particular moment.

People buy from a brand based on what comes to the front of their mind when they decide to buy something: preference, online research, friends' recommendations, aesthetics amongst many things. You should market your brand by building relationships on social media without trying to sell, with a view to becoming a 'top-of-mind' purchase.

Building awareness and a relationship can be as simple as being less corporate and more friendly on social networks. This attitude needs to extend to all areas of customer interaction. I maintain my personal, conversational tone on social networks and in my weekly newsletter so that a couple of times I have had people reply and ask 'Did you write that email specifically to me?'

If you can't handle the volume of messages your business gets, hire more staff and create an auto-response that helps to direct people with urgent issues and lets them know when (and if) to expect a direct response.

By letting people know they matter, you start to matter to them. If you don't have a brand, you have no way to create mass customer loyalty. In all you do, work to win prospective customers' affection.

TO HIT THE MONEY SPOT™
remember that your brand extends beyond aesthetics to how you treat people and make them feel. The way customers feel about you is more important than anything because if they can feel your love, they'll love you back.

MARKETING

1

Love Your Customers

In the last chapter I talked about doing things that ensure customers' affection for your brand increases.

'Loving your customers' is a little different; it's about how you feel about your customers.

It might seem natural that you would love people who are purchasing products from you – this is not necessarily so, as I found out in one of my businesses.

I'm going to come straight out and say it. When I started coaching people on how to get a job in investment banking I rapidly discovered that I didn't like many of the male clients.

Having been fortunate to work with genuinely great people in banking I thought the cliché of aggressive, self-important bankers was a myth – but it is not. There were many reasons I disliked these guys: they were self-righteous, they were extremely entitled and not very grateful for their position in life; they wanted to get so much back for doing very little, they were for the most part disgustingly money-driven.

The women were the complete opposite. They were gracious, polite and never inconsiderate of my time. They were a pleasure to help and work with.

I continued trying to coach both men and women, but in the end I stopped coaching men – our principles didn't fit.

Ultimately, if you don't like your clientele you will find it not only hard to work for them but you will not enjoy it. This might come through in the quality of your work.

If there are certain customers you definitely don't enjoy working with, consider having a business partner or colleague deal with them; or perhaps it could be time to pivot into a new business.

Research suggests that people not only prefer to buy from brands they think highly of but brands they believe think highly of them.

Why do you think artists, creatives and people who are generally different love Apple products? One reason is that Apple's Steve Jobs came right out and said I love you guys. See this famous quote:

'Here's to the crazy ones, the misfits, the rebels, the troublemakers, the round pegs in the square holes... the ones who see things differently – they're not fond of rules. You can quote them, disagree with them, glorify or vilify them, but the only thing you can't do is ignore them because they change things; they push the human race forward, and while some may see them as the crazy ones, we see genius, because the ones who are crazy enough to think that they can change the world, are the ones who do.'

STEVE JOBS

If you feel you are a misfit, and many people think that they are indeed different, you would have immediate affection for the Apple brand because the head of the company just said he thinks you're cool. He thinks you're the reason the world progresses, he thinks you're a genius. Why wouldn't you support a company that thinks so highly of you?

Another example shows the opposite: in the 1991 Gerald Ratner owned a thriving jewelry chain. Two statements he made brought his business to its knees in days. During a speech he proclaimed:

'People say 'How can you sell this for such a low price?'. I say 'because it's total crap.' To add insult to injury he was also

caught saying that some of the earrings his chain sold were *'Cheaper than an M&S [supermarket] prawn sandwich but probably wouldn't last as long.'*

By showing such contempt and a lack of concern for his customers £500m ($900m) was wiped off the value of his company in days. Close to collapse Ratner resigned and the business had to be completely renamed and rebranded to dissociate itself from him and his unfortunate statements.

TO HIT THE MONEY SPOT™
*you need to be genuinely
into the people you
are trying to serve.*

2

Blog Weekly, No Excuses

Blogging is one of the simplest and cheapest ways to build an audience and to bring traffic to your site. If your website consists of just a few informational pages plus your webstore, very few people will land there via google searches. Importantly, you won't have much in the way of click bait to post on social networks.

The problem with blogging is that most people aren't consistent. Apparently up to 90% of bloggers quit within six months of starting. If you want your blog to become successful in bringing people to your site you need to keep these 10 pointers in mind.

1 Consistency is key. This is the single most important tip I can give you. You need to keep producing content, week in, week out. At least in the first year, you shouldn't have even a single week when you don't post something to your blog. If you're planning a holiday write a few blogs in advance.

2 Passion helps. If you're really into what you're writing about then it will be easy to write. Some bloggers fail because they start for the wrong reason. Blogging to make money is not a good reason if you have no passion for the topic you're writing about. You won't be able to keep it up. It will feel like a huge chore.

3 Volume matters. If you have a blog or are planning one you've probably thought about how many posts per week are enough. I can give you a definitive answer. At least <u>five a week</u> is a good number if you're going to make a dent in your field rapidly. The likelihood is that someone else has already been writing on your topic for years and for that reason they are very well indexed by Google; if you want to be seen as an authority or expert website by Google you need to catch up. When I started my hair blog *NenoNatural.com* I stuck to at least five blogs of at least 500 words each a week. This means I had about 260 blogs by year end or about 130,000 words. If another hair blogger averaged one blog per week they would have had only 26,000 words on their website. In the eyes of search engines I would be the bigger authority on the topic.

4 Smart titles bring traffic. Give your blog posts titles with keywords that people will actually be searching. I started my very first blog during the Christmas of 2006; it was more like an online diary. Free blogging sites like *Blogger* weren't a thing yet so I had to learn html. I learned just enough to build my own website and started blogging. Because I wasn't writing with an audience in mind, many of my titles were creative and obscure, designed to make me look smart rather than to be found by search engines. The site, unsurprisingly, never got many hits. When I started blogging to attract an audience I learned how to write more search-engine-friendly titles; you should do the same. Use Google's Keyword Planner to help you write titles. A great way to start is to write titles that you think people will actually be typing into Google's search engine.

5 The social networks are key. Posting links to your social networks will increase your website traffic multiple times over. If you're a savvy social networker most of your website traffic can be generated from your networks rather than through Google searches. The smart way to use social networks: use a tool to syndicate your content to the social networks, e.g. HootSuite and SproutSocial. Preset posts to go out when your audience is actually awake. I post at least hourly on Twitter and at least twice daily on Facebook – more than this could be perceived as spam. I post daily on Pinterest and Instagram too.

6 Unitary focus helps. It's extremely hard to build an audience based around a life blog even if you are super interesting. Even super interesting people usually focus on one aspect of their lives to blog or vlog about. To build a target audience you need to blog about your specific niche topic. Mine is kinky and curly hair. My blog started off as a diary and I maintain a life section to this day and another section on books I read. These sections are not promoted much, I generally stick to sharing my hair blogs on social media. Unitary focus helps because when people think of your niche you want them to think about you. If you write about everything under the sun then you're not really associated with one particular thing. Your brand becomes diluted.

7 Quality matters. If your blog is full of typos, the font is too small or the colors make it hard to read readers won't spend much time on it. It's that simple.

A study by Canadian researchers published in the journal, *Behaviour and Information Technology*, found that people make their decision about whether they like a website in a 20th of a second; basically, in the blink of an eye. Not only that, this first impression lasts a long time and impacts the decision of whether or not to revisit the site.

8 Email collection is pertinent. A successful website collects emails. If a website visitor likes your content or whatever you promise to consistently deliver enough to leave their email, then you're doing something right. Your entire website needs to be geared towards encouraging people to want you in their inbox.

9 A great tone keeps people reading. I always write in a conversational tone, even for academic work. If you write in a chatty tone your blog will be easier to read and more relatable. Trying to sound too clever can alienate many potential readers.

10 Inspirational features will catapult your success. NenoNatural.com promotes those with kinky and curly hair by posting inspirational features of their hair journeys. Many people have very interesting hair stories or just want to show off their beautiful hair. This input encourages visitors to the blog to look for new hair styles or simply to read other people's stories.

Many of those featured at NenoNatural.com/queens have large followings themselves. Being featured on NenoNatural.com is exclusive; every entry, especially submitted images, have to meet a quality standard, so we don't accept everyone. The results of adding a features section were extraordinary: it had taken 15 months to grow to 120,000 Facebook fans. Over the next five months we grew to 280,000 Facebook fans. I can't say with certainty that the features were the main reason but it was the only thing we were doing differently when Facebook growth blew up.

TO HIT THE MONEY SPOT™
you need to be consistent and strategic about blogging. Blogging is not an option, it's a necessity for online success.

3

Email Your Fans For A Weekly Chat

An email list is pure gold. Most people check their emails several times a day and are very precious about what lands in their inbox. When people are no longer interested in what you have to say, they usually unsubscribe or hit spam in which case your email manager should automatically unsubscribe them.

An email address is much more important than interacting on social networks for three key reasons:

1 With email you have a larger degree of control over when you send content to targeted readers. You can more easily subdivide your list into groups, e.g. by country, leading to more effective interaction. The social networks, notably Facebook, change their rules regularly; usually in their favor and against your interests. To get exposure on Facebook now you have to keep paying to boost posts even if you paid to grow your page in the first place. It really is atrocious behavior but they have us exactly where they want us, by the short and curlies.

2 Only your most interested fans will give you an email

address. Email is where all our important stuff goes, passwords, messages from mum, dad, friends and so on. This self-selecting group of people is really saying: 'I'm letting you into my personal space,' because that's what email is – personal real estate online. Many secrets lie in inboxes.

3 Emails are always seen. We all miss posts on Twitter, Instagram and Facebook but every email, even if we choose not to read it, is seen as we scan our Inbox for important messages. Even if a reader chooses to delete or not open a message, they probably saw it and it's up to you to write better subject lines so more of your emails are opened.

On some level, email is less powerful than it used to be because people sign up to so many things, but it's still the only piece of customer information you have some of degree of control over. The fact that it's lower impact just means that it cannot be the only way you interact with your fans.

An email list is the single most important marketing tool. It allows you to know who your biggest fans are and how to reach them. In addition to being present on social networks, you *must* start to build an email list from the very beginning.

So, how do we build that list? I have some very practical tips for you on this; having built a list of 30,000 subscribers in about a year and half, I have good experience.

Firstly, building an effective email list requires work; it's not easy. I completely failed to build a list of any significance in two earlier businesses because I didn't know the stuff I'm about to share with you.

The most effective tool I have found for email list building is **creating a freebie**, like a free ebook, a free white paper or free software. Free gifts don't always work, mind you, but if you create something your niche really wants, with an effective title, it will work.

Whatever your freebie is, make sure it is crammed with helpful advice or is highly useful. This will help to cement people's trust in you.

These are the 10 commandments of email list building:

1 Don't buy email lists, only deal with opt-ins

Not only is buying emails illegal in many countries now, a bought email list is almost completely ineffective. If spam filters don't catch it, the recipient will probably report it as spam or simply ignore it. Most people don't take kindly to unsolicited emails; I know for sure my initial reaction is irritation and you're never going to get a positive reaction out of someone you've just irritated.Remember that your website and social media are not the only platforms through which you can collect email addresses. If you host a seminar or other live event, make sure to have a signup sheet asking people for their emails so you can get in touch afterwards. If you attend a trade show, have a business card box. Tell people to throw their business cards in to keep in touch. Even better, run a raffle and tell people who stop at your booth that they stand to win something if they throw their business card in. The better the prize, the more likely people will volunteer their business cards. Don't forget to state you will be adding them to your list otherwise it's not an opt-in.

2 Use an email management tool, e.g. MailChimp.com

Email management software automates the email process, stops you from getting blocked by spam filters and allows people to unsubscribe easily.

Other email management tools include: Aweber (probably the most longstanding), Infusionsoft, ConstantContact, iContact, and GetResponse. New email management tools are coming out all the time. Email software can capture details you couldn't even dream of capturing if you tried to do things manually, such as location, email client (yahoo, gmail etc) and the type of device (PC, mobile etc) the subscriber uses. This data is automatically created with no extra effort on your part.

3 Embed the email form in many places on your website

I only ask subscribers to provide their first name and an email as compulsory inputs. All other information they choose to give me is optional. Overall, the less you ask for, the more likely people are to enter their details. A first name allows you to personalize emails.

Think about using one or all of these strategies:

- Include a link encouraging people to subscribe to your email list at the end of every blog post; highlighting your free gift to maximize the number of opt-ins
- Have a 'subscribe now' pop-up appear every time your website gets a new visitor
- Have a squeeze page or a subscriber wall. A squeeze page is a one-page website designed to maximize email opt-ins. When a new person arrives at the website, they can't see any of the information available unless they subscribe. Or they can see a very limited amount of the content.

The squeeze page will normally have some great copy, or

testimonials and a promotional video to encourage the web visitor to volunteer their information.

4 Get people clicking through to your email list by posting a link on social networks

Embedding a MailChimp sign-up form on Facebook is easy. However, people might not see it; at times I add a link to my subscription page when I post pretty pictures on social media.

5 Keep emails short, clear and information-rich

No one has the time or patience to read more than 300 to 500 words in a single sitting. If your emails are long and dull, you'll get more unsubscribes.

6 Monitor email frequency

I think a daily email is too much unless you are providing *very* valuable, can't-live-without, time-sensitive information, e.g. your baby day-by-day when a woman is pregnant. Two to three times a week is probably too much for most types of business. I email my list weekly; I used to do it twice a week but changed my mind after monitoring unsubscribe rates. Don't go more than a month without contacting your email list so that people don't forget you! However, have something useful to say otherwise you will get a lot of unsubscribes.

Sending emails out on a regular basis will help to keep the list fresh because email management software cleans up emails that no longer exist and people who are no longer interested in your content opt-out. It will also keep you at the top of people's minds.

7 Gain Trust

Be honest. Don't mis-sell your products. Don't sell in every email. In fact sell very subtly using an effective, graphic header. Share information about yourself. One of the best tips I ever received from Jim Cockrum on writing emails was 'to write to my mother.' If you write an email as though you are writing to one person you make it more personal and much more relatable.

8 Don't spam, ever

Do NOT keep posting links to your sign-up form on your Facebook page or other social forums. People will get annoyed because they hate being 'sold' to. I have 'unfollowed' the odd tweeter or Facebook page because they are overdoing their marketing.

9 Learn from others

Every time an email you receive convinces you to buy something, consider what about that campaign convinced you. Use the same strategy for sculpting your own emails.

10 Write awesome subject lines

The single biggest factor impacting whether or not people open your emails is the subject line. If it promises something interesting then people will open and read what's inside. Journalists spend ages coming up with headlines that get people's attention. Nowadays we have websites so specialized in getting clicks through captivating titles leading to that now common phrase click bait. The biggest culprits in neglecting to build an email list are new-age YouTube celebrities, especially the accidental ones. They forget that it is not their platform and building their own email and customer list is crucial for their longevity. YouTube can change their rules or their freemium model in a heartbeat so it's not a good idea to be over-reliant on the status quo.

TO HIT THE MONEY SPOT™
*collect emails and maintain
a regular and friendly
discussion with your
biggest fans.*

4

Vlog To Build Deeper Connections

Video is the most intimate way to communicate with an audience. People who consistently choose to watch your videos actually like you, your voice and your delivery. This makes a YouTube audience a very dedicated and loyal fan base compared to fans on other social networks.

If you grow a big enough audience people will want to have access to it; they will ask you to review or introduce a product to them. In a product review, you tell your audience what you like about the product, what you might like improved and perhaps compare it to similar products that you've used. In a product introduction, you explain how a product works, what it looks like and where your fans can get it.

YouTube is the biggest video platform by a long shot and I very much doubt anyone will kick them off that pedestal in the foreseeable future. When I first started making videos I also used Vimeo; it completely paled in comparison. YouTube allows you to upload an unlimited number of videos for free and they share advertising revenue with you. Vimeo limits upload volumes and charges you for going over – why they think that model can compete with YouTube's, I do not know.

No one was watching my Vimeo videos so I ditched the platform after a couple of months.

So, how do you build this audience anyway?

I did it by uploading interesting videos to YouTube on a specific genre or related genres.

My YouTube channel is actually an accident. I created it way back in 2007 to watch videos and used my username from work, *hkatsonga*, as my YouTube username. At the time, the thought that I would ever upload videos to the internet was not even a consideration.

In 2011, I decided to teach my husband, Harry, my native language, Chichewa, and we started uploading videos to the channel. The videos were very niche and we were only uploading them on to there as a personal video database and to give my sister in the US a laugh. Lo and behold, people started watching the videos. It was exciting to have a bit of an audience but it was still just for fun. I worked in banking at the time. By the end of our first year uploading to YouTube the channel had 43 subscribers and 10,529 total channel views.

Eighteen months into uploading language videos I decided to start uploading hair videos (mid 2012, just after I quit banking). Although this was still a hobby, I decided I wouldn't upload anymore language videos to the channel because hair and the Chichewa language were completely unrelated. I was also starting to get bored of the language videos.

I uploaded 22 hair videos to the channel over the next six months.

By the end of the second year the channel had 213 subscribers and 39,030 total channel views. I had quit my job six months before and I was starting to think seriously about how I could use YouTube to grow NenoNatural.com, the hair hobby I had just decided to convert into a business.

So, we're now in 2013, the third year of uploading video content to the internet, and I'm thinking, what can I do to grow this audience? I decided to upload two videos a week, every week, and to improve their quality. I already had a good camera so I bought better lighting.

Instead of uploading only what I wanted to upload, I started looking at similar channels and seeing which videos got more views. I went from uploading what I wanted to what my audience wanted to watch. This simple flip in mindset revealed two interesting things: my audience weren't just interested in my hair videos, they were more interested in my life! Secondly, they loved videos where my husband made a cameo appearance.

I had been nervous about getting too personal on videos because I wasn't sure there would be much interest, but viewers were always asking me to reveal more. I gave in; towards the end of year three my husband and I uploaded a video on how we met – the response was phenomenal, the video became my most watched within weeks. I already had about 150 videos on my channel so for this one upload to shoot to the top of the charts so quickly was a sign: get personal.

Year Three ended with 4,173 subscribers (subbies) and over 245,000 channel views. This was a spectacular result especially considering six months before we only had about 600 subbies even after doing a giveaway that required a subscription to YouTube. We were officially getting somewhere.

I decided I would start mixing videos on hair with videos about our daily life featuring, *The Good Husband,* as I started calling my husband Harry in videos. In Year Four we had our first baby and shared that journey too.

TO HIT THE MONEY SPOT™

grow a loyal following using videos. Upload consistently, focus on a narrow range of topics and listen to what your audience wants rather than what you want.

5

The Smart Way To Get Your Content Out To Hundreds of Fans

Content is key. I hope this message has come out loud and clear throughout the book so far. However, there is something even more important that content: distribution. The more you distribute your content in places where people are, the more traffic you will get back to your site. Social media is a key content distribution platform.

Social media is fun but it can also be a time vortex. Even the most disciplined of souls can struggle to extract themselves from chatting on Facebook, Twitter or whichever medium you prefer; falling for click bait and taking random tests (e.g. *Which celebrity are you?*) or watching what ends up being hours of funny or sad videos. **Fact: fun things are hard to ignore or stop doing.**

To make the most of social media posting and cut down the time you spend on it, you need to use a tool that can automate your posts. This is not cheating or inauthentic provided you follow three rules:

1 You or your social media manager should write all the posts to ensure they are high quality. If people don't value what you are sharing you won't get many followers

2 Log onto your social networks periodically to see who is interacting with you: asking questions, making comments and sharing. Social media is not a one-way conversation. Interaction is necessary for it to be effective

3 Don't keep posting the same content over and over again. If your feed is too repetitive people will get bored or annoyed and unsubscribe, unfollow or unlike you

Automating is easy to implement if you are a prolific content creator. Whenever I write a blog, or periodically if I don't have time, after writing blogs for a few weeks I collect all the tweetable lines out of my blog posts as well as a link to the post and keep it in a spreadsheet. This means I have a ready supply of posts to upload.

I then use my preferred automation tool, Gremln, to bulk upload all my posts to various social networks.

I now have so many tweetables saved that, even though I tweet once every hour, I don't need to repeat any one tweet more than twice a year and I can upload a whole year of hourly tweets within a few minutes. I normally only post a month's worth of tweets so that I can change my social media strategy each month.

By automating your posts in this way you can post when your audience are actually online without having to be online at the same time. I literally post whilst I sleep. Then, at some point everyday I log on to the networks and respond to everyone who's been asking questions and making comments.

Image-based posts

People love pictorial posts from any beauty business they choose to follow because they inspire their own beauty routine or household décor. NenoNatural.com receives hundreds of pictures weekly from people who want to be featured on our social networks and blog so I always have a wealth of pictures to post. You can find software for posting images too.

I have a marketing assistant who posts pretty images to Pinterest, Twitter and Instagram almost daily. I prefer to have an actual human being doing this work; we only post the best quality images and a human being needs to decide which ones are good enough to be used.

There is no way we could post all the images we receive; we get far too many.

The beauty of running a beauty-based social media page is that to all your fans it's a hobby. They will want to engage with you on holiday, during breaks, work hours, weekends – basically, all the time including on Christmas day, I kid you not.

The fact that your business is a hobby or fun thing to fans and followers means it is very easy to get engagement. In addition, you can make many more posts without being reported for spam. In fact, for us beauty business owners, the business is also a hobby – or at least it should be – that's why it's so easy to spend more time than you should on social media.

New software for pre-setting social media posts are popping up all the time. I have tried and didn't like Hootsuite, probably the most popular (I personally do not get the hype, if you do – call me), as well as ping.fm, now called Seesmic.

Different tools do different things: some handle text only or images only, others both text and images; some can work with more social networks than others – most can only post to Facebook, Twitter and LinkedIn whilst others will syndicate to many more networks. A few specializing in Pinterest posts have cropped up.

Whatever the case, make sure you choose a tool that can handle bulk uploads. This is the key to efficient distribution.

Social media efficiency and automation tools you can look at include:

* BufferApp.com
* Crowdbooster.com
* EveryPost.me
* Gremln.com
* HootSuite.com
* Posts.so
* Seesmic.com
* SocialOomph.com
* Spredfast.com
* SproutSocial.com
* SocialFlow.com
* ViralTag.com

Personally, I think some of these tools are completely overpriced. Do some proper research before you settle on one.

TO HIT THE MONEY SPOT™

automate your social media posts and manage the amount of time you spend on social media. If you do not have a social media strategy you will waste lots of unnecessary time.

6

Get A Magazine Gig

According to *Brainfluence* by Roger Dooley, people who see content in a hard copy format absorb more of it and retain it for a longer period of time. This implies that a printed advert leaves a stronger imprint on someone's memory than an identical digital advert. This is one of the reasons I like to have some presence in a printed magazine.

Writing for a magazine also comes with some kudos. In order to get a magazine column you need to be of a certain stature – it automatically gives you a mark of authority on your subject.

I was very lucky to be asked to write for a magazine for the first time. They approached me when I only had 5,000 likes because their founder had seen one of my posts and liked it. It also helped that I had a decent following because I would obviously let my fans know that I had written an article on such and such whenever a new edition came out. The magazine was printed quarterly so producing content was not too much of a strain on my time. I wrote for free in return for some exposure.

Incidentally, I was approached by another magazine at the same time but within less than five minutes of skimming through their website I was not interested. The website was shoddy and the magazine they sent me was very poorly typeset. Be careful to choose an imprint that you'll be proud to have your name associated with.

So, how can you get your own magazine gig? It's quite simple: approach magazines.

Tender your interest by sending an email or letter stating who you are, what makes you an authority on the subject you want to write about and what sort of social media following you have. Magazines want people with a big following as columnists because it extends their own reach.

To increase your chances of getting a response, write to small magazines, new ones and local ones. If you pitch too high you won't get a response. I wrote to the likes of Ebony and Essence in the US and I got zilch. I was small fish to them (at the time), so they weren't interested. I hadn't even reached 100,000 fans on Facebook so I was definitely being over-optimistic, as so many hair bloggers were already a lot bigger than I was.

If you don't receive a response the first time, write again. Phone in.

In another business I got a writing gig by engaging with the editor on Twitter. Within just a couple of months of joining the social network, I got some of the blogs I had written on my site girlbanker.com published on the leading recruitment editorial eFinancialCareers. How did this happen?

I simply retweeted and commented on something the editor had said. Interested by my comment the editor clicked through to my website using the link on my Twitter description page. She liked what she saw so she asked if she could use some of my posts. This was not a planned marketing strategy for me, it just happened. It was like a dream. If I had written a list of blogs to target, this would have been at the very top of that list.

Whichever social networks you join, be on the lookout for similar opportunities to connect with thought leaders.

Incidentally, the day after I wrote the first draft of this chapter I received an email from a magazine in Ghana stating they were happy to print articles written by me. It came as surprise because I had written to them seven months earlier and had not heard back since.

TO HIT THE MONEY SPOT™
*it helps to raise your profile
and authority by writing
for credible magazines
within your niche.*

7

Get A Newspaper Gig

Having your name in a newspaper is another mark of social approval. You want to be featured in the broadsheets rather than the tabloids; the wider the newspaper's coverage, the better. Even if you don't get any leads from the feature you can now say 'As Featured In'…

I have written for two national newspapers in my time: I wrote a weekly personal finance and business advice column targeted at women for *Malawi News*. The editor approached me because she'd heard I was knowledgeable in matters related to money. I wrote for 18 months before I resigned. NenoNatural.com was growing rapidly and I couldn't maintain the commitment any longer.

I then wrote a weekly column on curly hair for Ghana's biggest national newspaper *The Daily Graphic*. I got this position in the way described in the above chapter. I just wrote to them. You're probably wondering, why Ghana? I'm not from there and I have never even been there; it was one of four countries in Africa that I wanted to get into with my products. I wrote letters to a couple of newspapers and magazines in my target countries, threw a couple of free pens into the envelopes and waited.

I only wrote to two imprints in Ghana: *The Daily Graphic* responded within two weeks and I wrote for about three months before I decided it was a strain on my time. *Agoo*, the magazine I wrote to, responded seven months later. Two out of two means I had a 100% conversion rate for Ghana.

An online media site in Nigeria also accepted my proposal but in the end they didn't print the first column I wrote for them and I didn't follow it up. I definitely could have been more strategic about managing these partnerships but I was still working on my own and I was taking too much on.

I received three responses from eight letters but I could have confirmed five or six if I had been more persistent in my efforts by following up.

Ultimately, I learned that getting space in newspapers and magazines is achievable. Once your business grows large enough, take on a dedicated writer (part-time or full-time) who writes all your sales copy and articles for other media sites.

You don't have to do all your own writing. Articles can be printed as being written by the company rather than as by you, the owner of the company.

Writing letters is a lot less scary than getting on the phone. To maximize the likelihood that your letters will be read, write to a person within the company rather than to generic departments. Generic letters will just get lost in the chaos of daily office life.

TO HIT THE MONEY SPOT™
it helps to raise your profile
and authority by writing
for a national or local
newspapers; the bigger the
better.

8

Partner Up

You can't add your way to millions, you need to multiply.

Don't operate within a silo. Continually seek to connect with other people in your niche to form mutually-beneficial partnerships. I follow several high-profile internet marketers and I have seen that they do this. When one writes a book, others promote it for them to their fan base, knowing that when they write a book they will receive the same favor.

Partnerships obviously extend well beyond book launches. You can ask other players in your niche to share something you are working on with their email list and you can similarly share their work with yours.

Partnerships have to be balanced. If you have an email list of 5,000 people you can't really expect someone with an email list of 50,000 people to want to help you for free. You have to incentivize them with a generous share in affiliate income or pay a fee for the privilege of that exposure.

If and when you start selling physical products you will also want to form partnerships with shops so that they sell your products.

Think of innovative ways of partnering with others. Offer free exposure or connect people to resources that they need and you have. Take-up will probably be slow at first but with persistence and consistency, things will pick up.

When we started featuring people on NenoNatural.com (this is a form of partnering up), I hired my first part-time employee. I hired her through Elance (now called Upwork™) and she initially worked daily for a total of 20 hours a week.

In addition to picture marketing, she managed the whole feature section of the blog. She asked people to feature on our site – I gave her a request template. When people sent their profiles through she checked that all the questions had been answered and the pictures were of a high enough quality.

We allowed people to include links to all their social networks and if they had a YouTube channel we allowed them to include a video in the feature.

It was a win-win situation. They won because they got exposure on a website that was now getting up to 10,000 hits per day. NenoNatural.com won because we had a lot more content to post to the website. Many people we featured had a very decent following themselves so an unexpected benefit was that when we featured them they went and told their hundreds or even thousands of followers about it.

In trying to build a mutually-beneficial partnership think carefully about what you will offer the other party. Time is limited, so you are only going to get people's time and attention because it benefits them.

To fully understand how much most people love themselves read *How To Win Friends and Influence People* by Dale Carnegie. People will want to partner with you if you make them look good or make them money – if you can do both, more power to you.

TO HIT THE MONEY SPOT™
pursue and cement effective partnerships. Speak to prospective partners in terms of their wants, interests and motivations. This will produce the best response when pitching ideas or selling.

9

Customer Service Matters

OK, now I'm getting really corporate with terms like 'customer service.' I don't want you to think of customers in the cliché way – all smiles, *would you like fries with that* and *have a nice day*. It's pretty simple: what perception do you want to leave with people who interact with you and your business.

A lot of customer service nowadays is pretty insincere and exaggerated. It's a lot better to be yourself and leave the customer feeling they have had a genuine interaction with you.

Customer service applies to every single interaction that a person has with your business: your website, your products, getting a response when they encounter a problem, responses to emails and social media interactions. Everyone that works for you and on your behalf should understand your brand values and the impression you like to leave with customers and prospects.

Ultimately, be nice.

Whenever you interact think, 'I want to make the customer happy,' not 'I want to save money.' If you do everything possible to make the customer happy, profits will surely follow.

One annoyed customer can lose you lots of business nowadays because social media spreads the rate at which bad news travels. You should rather lose a bit of money than have even one fan make a negative social post about you or your business.

Importantly, make a plan for when you are too big to respond to emails yourself. Once your content gains traction you will not be able to cope with the volume; you'll need an assistant or two for sure. Give your assistant a framework for responding to emails.

My virtual assistant responds in her name but because I have a fun, dynamic personality I ask her to portray the same characteristics when she responds to emails. My personality is part of my brand. I'm all about sharing positive energy.

TO HIT THE MONEY SPOT™
treat every single customer
and potential customer like
they mean the world to you.
Ensure all your staff and
support services do the same.

DISTRIBUTION

1

Forget Your Own Website

Yes, you do absolutely need a website. It's very odd for a business in this day and age to not have at least a rudimentary one. However, don't expect it to generate huge sales.

Especially if you are a new brand with a small or non-existent social following, sales conversions from your own site will be low.

Even if your brand is huge online – on YouTube or elsewhere – shoppers are likely to prefer shopping on existing platforms such as Amazon or eBay.

When it comes to sales, Amazon is the king. According to a 2013 Forbes article, sales on Amazon exceed the total of the next 12 biggest online sites, including Target and Walmart. If you position yourself correctly you can do very well on Amazon.

eBay is also a great platform depending on what products you are selling. All online retail sales platforms have their own unique features and feel so you should focus on setting one up properly before moving on to another platform.

Should you start off on eBay or on Amazon? I prefer Amazon; my brother prefers eBay. We both generate six-figures in annual sales. He thinks Amazon is complicated, too expensive and generally just unfair to sellers. I think eBay still has that second-hand product feel and the products that I sell, premium products, look better on Amazon.

However, my preference is insignificant compared to how prospective customers shop.

Prospective buyers shop in a particular way. They buy something because they prefer it, they think of it (i.e. it's at the top of their mind due to advertising etc) or research suggests it will suit their needs best. Where they buy it is probably where they usually go for that type of purchase.

Unless it's an unusual item most shoppers are unlikely to look for a new place to purchase it from. This is why you want to be on popular retail sites.

What Influences Where You Buy Something?

Convenience

If something is available on Amazon as well as the seller's website you will probably go to Amazon. Why? Perhaps because you are already familiar with how the purchase process on Amazon works or because your credit card details are already on the site so buying is much faster. If you have Amazon Prime you get rapid, free delivery.

On the other hand, if you always buy that type of thing on eBay then you would go straight to eBay.

As a seller, I have a strong preference for Amazon but as a buyer I would have to say I use them both equally. In fact, sometimes I enjoy shopping on eBay a lot more than I do on Amazon. There are some things I always buy on eBay and others that I always buy on Amazon.

Perceived Safety

A buyer might feel that their payment details are safer with a large retailer than a small one. Of course, if a hacker wants to cause maximum damage, they will target a big, powerful retailer rather than a small online outfit.

Brand

Generally, if something goes wrong with a purchase we all take comfort in the fact that a brand, small or large, with a significant reputation online and elsewhere will do anything in their power to correct the error. The result is that we're more likely to buy from known brands. This is why you need to work towards having the status of an established, well-known brand.

TO HIT THE MONEY SPOT™
*accept that your own
website is much less
important than sales on
online giant retail sites. To
get ahead you need to claim
your spot on Amazon, eBay
or both.*

2

Your Time Is Way Too Precious For Posting And Packing

I'm very much pro a flexible lifestyle with more play than work.

Whilst I accept that the first few years as a start-up are hard work and involve a lot of ungodly hours, the goal is to do less and less work over time. You want to get to a level where four hours per day, five days a week is all your business needs from you.

Once you have everything up and running, with all core products rolled out, you want to delegate and contract out. You don't need to hire an army of employees to run a large outfit.

Fulfillment is a third-party service I recommend you use from the start. You might grow so large that you decide to bring fulfillment in-house but when you're starting out this will save you lots of time and capital.

First things first, what is fulfillment?

A fulfillment house is a company that stores your product(s) in their warehouses and whenever an order is received, they pack and ship the item to the buyer. For efficiency you need to connect your fulfillment house to your webstore and your Amazon or eBay site so that orders automatically flow through to them with no required action from you.

Fulfillment houses can charge for some or all of the below. Some of the charges are per hour, others per item:

* Receiving merchandise
* Storage, either per item or according to the size of the pallet you deliver to them
* Processing payments
* The cost of shipping to customers
* Picking and packing your product(s)
* Processing product returns
* Preparing documentation for international shipments
* Providing reports to you, the merchant
* Making bank deposits
* Answering customer queries

You can opt out of certain services, e.g. customer service.

Some fulfillment houses will only deal with clients of a certain size. However, with Amazon now in the fulfillment business many providers have lost a lot of business and are more flexible on size. Amazon deals with sellers of all sizes, tiny and huge; they also accept a wide range of products; they will take almost anything on.

Fulfillment is the reason you don't need to quit your day job too soon!

I love the fulfillment business. When I started producing products for NenoNatural.com, a lot of business was coming from the US. I didn't want customers to wait a week or more to receive their orders, so within two months I was using Fulfillment by Amazon in the US.

I did shop around the different fulfillment houses but, ultimately, I was convinced that Amazon would be the best option to start off with because I was already selling on the Amazon platform. Since then I have tried another fulfillment house. They had lower fees for picking and packing than Amazon but they couldn't beat the Amazon experience so I stopped using them after a few months.

For instance, on Amazon your customers can get free shipping without you being charged back whereas all other fulfillment house charge shipping back to you. Amazon works 24-7 so your customers get their orders fast; Amazon also provides a lot of data to sellers; the company breaks all costs down so everything is fully transparent. I haven't found any other fulfillment house that can provide that much data.

Amazon charges lower fees to sellers who use several of their services (e.g. selling and fulfillment rather than just selling) so I find the service cost-effective and time-efficient too.

Hiring a fulfillment house is tantamount to having a whole army ready and waiting to pack and ship your goods.

Posting and packing products is neither enjoyable nor a good use of your time. You need to apply yourself to those tasks that need *your* brain to generate business growth. You could train anyone to do your posting and packing in two days, releasing your time for more specialized and creative tasks.

Search Google for 'fulfillment service in {country}' to find the perfect fulfillment service business for you.

eBay Fulfillment

If you live in the US and don't want to deal with the documentation required for international orders you can use eBay's fulfillment platform.

This is how it works: when you get an international order rather than shipping it abroad you ship it to eBay at the usual domestic cost and they ship it abroad for you.

I have raved about Amazon a great deal here but I have to admit that their size scares me. At the end of the day, Amazon own their platform and if they are not happy with your performance for any reason, they can and they will boot you off. The larger Amazon gets, the more power they will have to bully sellers. For this reason, I recommend diversifying your sales. Once you are doing well on Amazon, branch off to other platforms.

If your products are well-branded, you will develop a loyal following. If you were to be booted off Amazon, the most dedicated would look for your website. Ensure that as you grow on Amazon you download your customer's details to your own hard drive. Amazon don't make this easy. Your buyer database is where your business's value lies.

Encourage buyers to subscribe to your email list using offers included with purchases.

TO HIT THE MONEY SPOT™

pass all manual, operational tasks such as order fulfillment to third-party contractors. Spend the extra time building your brand and on marketing efforts.

3

Forget Supermarkets

It's the dream isn't it? To have a big chain stock your products? Well, yes and no. There are things about being stocked in a supermarket that make them very unattractive.

There is a good reason you don't have premium brands like MAC makeup in supermarkets. Large chain supermarkets lend themselves much more to generic, low-margin, value products. If you desperately want to get into a supermarket chain and have been thinking this is easy to do then I hate to be the bearer of bad news but to small suppliers supermarkets are bullies.

Supermarkets are in business to bring your pricing to its knees so that they can make their profit. Quality is a foregone conclusion to them. Even the biggest brands have to take their best negotiators to get a good partnership deal with a supermarket.

What does this mean? It means if you're selling a premium product you'll come out with a budget one – either immediately or in the long run.

Supermarket buyers are trained to win negotiations. They will do everything to make you feel inferior to them so that they get the most out of any deal. They are extremely tactical and use the best and latest psychology research to come out ahead.

They do things like keep you waiting because that in itself will start to make you feel nervous and more eager to strike any deal. Walmart's negotiating rooms are apparently down long unstimulating corridors and have tiny windows, all aimed at improving their negotiating power. In addition, you are placed in a small chair behind a massive desk, because research suggests this all contributes to their power over you.

If you are fortunate enough to pitch to a supermarket, go into that meeting believing that your product is the best thing since sliced bread; that *they* are lucky to be seeing you. Be prepared to walk away without a deal.

Get *Pitch Anything* by Oren Klaff to better understand the strategies you can use to win pitches. In addition, the terminology of the book will help you to better understand the power of supermarkets.

My contract manufacturer hates supermarkets. There is only one chain they have respect for, John Lewis / Waitrose who they have found to be more ethical in negotiating than the others. In their experience this is how dealing with supermarkets has impacted their brands:

You pitch your product. The supermarket, to make it 'worth their while', commits you to a Buy-One-Get-One-Free (BOGOF), period, two or three times a year. Whenever you see BOGOFs in a store they are funded by the supplier *not* the supermarket. This obviously slices your margin in half immediately. However, when BOGOF week arrives, they order three or four times the quantity due to expected higher demand.

You get paid half what you normally get per product. However, if that stock lasts beyond the promotional period (and it always does because they over-order), they keep the extra profit.

So, at the end of BOGOF week, prices are hiked back up to normal. Any unsold stock is sold at the regular price and the supermarket keeps all the extra profit.

What does it mean for you, the supplier? Well, what most suppliers normally do is dilute the product to avoid going bankrupt.

I have personally noticed a few new products fall in quality over time. I had a favorite rice pudding brand, because it was extremely rice-rich. A few months after it was introduced I noticed the rice density falling – there were only a few grains of rice per spoonful. I assumed the manufacturer was being unscrupulous and taking advantage of loyal fans. It sounds much more reasonable now that they were being squeezed by the supermarket. A couple of years later that brand has disappeared from some supermarkets' shelves.

As a new beauty brand I would recommend you ignore supermarkets either completely or until you are a big enough force to not care whether they take you on or not. Importantly, with online growing so rapidly, supermarkets are likely to become less arrogant.

TO HIT THE MONEY SPOT™
avoid supermarkets initially. They will bring your brand to its knees.

Get Into Specialist Stores And Specialist Locations

Whilst many supermarkets will likely result in a long-run win-lose for you, there are other outfits in the world of retail that are genuinely after a win-win: specialist stores and specialist locations.

Specialist shops

Compared to supermarkets, specialist shops, such as gift shops, will be much more considerate in negotiating payment schedules and reasonable pricing for your product. They want a win-win outcome because they need a continued wide and engaging range of products for their clientele; getting suppliers requires a little more work for them than it does for supermarkets.

I'm calling most places that aren't a supermarket a specialist shop. Supermarkets seek to serve everyone. Their strategy is to stock as many generic, low-margin goods as possible and turn over high volumes.

Specialist shops serve a niche customer. They would typically be much more interested in unique and curious goods for which they can charge a higher margin.

Hair and Beauty Product Shops

Many stores specialize in selling hair products. The US has a huge chain, Sally's, alongside all the smaller stores whereas Britain doesn't have a single large hair products chain. The largest chain has less than half a dozen stores.

Across Africa we also have many small stores that stock women's body products from hair and body potions to perfumes.

Specialist locations

Specialist *shops* sell merchandise, specialist *locations* primarily sell an experience. Places such as hair salons, spas, retreats, massage parlors and craft shops are there to provide an experience. Most specialist locations will have a suite of products that they upsell to their customers.

Hair Salons

After a stylist has just done someone's hair, they typically offer the products they have used on the client for sale. They might even go beyond that and offer accessories such as hair dryers, combs and hair straighteners. Pretty much anything to do with hair is fair game; if you have hair products or accessories, target hair salons.

Spas and Retreats

Spas and retreats sometimes offer body and bath products for sale. After you've had an amazing facial you're likely to be open to buying the take-home facial kits or any face creams that may have been used. If you're selling products that would sit well in a spa, retreat or massage parlor, get a list of locations and start prospecting.

Craft Shops

New DIY and craft shops are popping up all the time. Experiences I have had myself include a painting class in what was essentially a café and a pottery painting class in a café/deli.

The painting place wasn't savvy, they didn't upsell anything, but they were in a position to sell anything art-related. I was going art-crazy at the time. After the class I went to buy drawing pads, paints and even an easel that I haven't even used since.

The pottery shop sold you whatever piece of pottery you wanted to paint before you started the class.

These are just a couple of examples; the aim here is to make you think carefully about the type of places that might want your product. Hotels, for instance, may be interested in any sort of quirky linen or even furniture and interesting cushions.

Draw a mind map of the type of specialist / experience locations that your product would look good in or would complement the service of. Once you have an idea of what those places are, finding lists to start off with is usually quite simple using Google. If an online list is not available then a trade magazine with lots of contacts may be.

How Do You Get In?

Once you have a list of places where your product sits well, how do you go about getting your line stocked?

Firstly, don't pick up the phone just yet. There are a few things any retailer will ask you before they consider stocking your product and you need to know these before you jump onto the phone.

You need to prepare a product catalog for potential stockists or what some call a line sheet. This one-to-two page document includes:

* Your business contact details: name, address, website, email, phone number
* Your product line including available sizes, colors and styles
* Wholesale pricing (the price the retailer pays you)

- Recommended Retail Price, RRP (the price the specialist location or shop should ideally charge their customers for your products)
- Minimum order numbers –minimum orders for beauty products are usually in multiples of 6, 12 or 24
- Your USP (unique selling point) and your best selling products
- Samples if possible and images or video footage showing how your product looks and/or works if a sample cannot be brought to a meeting
- Any current stockists – this will validate you more than anything. It gives the seller comfort that they are not the first to 'take a risk' stocking your line
- If you can refer the seller to any independent online testimonials or features in popular media outlets, that will give you extra leverage to get in your product line in there
- Any other relevant details

TO HIT THE MONEY SPOT™

*consider all the specialist
retail shops and locations
that may want to stock
your product, design a
product catalog then write
a strategy for getting your
line into these shops.*

5

It's Time To Hone Your Negotiation Skills

Whenever you need to do something you have three options: do it yourself, get someone to do it for you or get help doing it. The more skills you develop the more you can deal with yourself especially if people let you down. There are a few skills you will have to improve regardless of which of these frameworks you opt for. Negotiation is one of those skills.

Getting products into stores requires you to negotiate contractual terms and conditions. You can usually get a lower price or more services for the same price. Some shops will not be open to negotiation but you have to at least try.

I have always loved haggling as a pastime so I try to get a deal even when it's nothing to do with business and no, I don't feel guilty about it at all. If there's a deal to be had, I'm having it.

The type of things you can get will shock you. I once called a well-known email service management company at 10 pm to get more information on their services. The package I wanted was $299 per month with 5,000 contacts included. The training package to understand the software was $1,999. By the time I was done I had 55,000 contacts on that package and I had slashed the cost of training to $999.

You would think I would be happy with this deal but by the very next day I was kicking myself for not getting a better one. Go figure.

How to Negotiate

Step 1: recognize when it's time to negotiate

The trigger to negotiate: even if a stockist hasn't confirmed that they will buy, they may indicate their interest by asking detailed questions about the product, pricing, demand etc.

Look out for any signals of interest.

Step 2: know what the stockist wants

Before you even start to negotiate you need to understand what the potential stockist wants. Fast-selling products at the best possible price.

There are some points in the year, month or week when stores are open to taking on new products. For instance, stocks for Christmas are determined many weeks in advance, many months for large stores. If you show up after a store has already finished negotiating products that will be stocked that Christmas you will likely get nowhere even if you feel there is plenty of time until Christmas.

Step 3: know what you want and when you will walk away

Besides price, there is a minimum level of service you will want, as well as the most convenient logistics possible.

For example, it's better for the store to keep you updated on stock levels rather than requiring you to check on stock levels yourself. Yes, some shops expect their suppliers to have people going round all the shops they sell to, ensuring there is enough stock.

Logistically, it's easier to have a store buy three months of stock at a time rather than purchasing weekly; it reduces your admin tasks. Of course, from a cash flow and warehousing perspective this may not be possible for many stores.

Step 4: be charming

Smile (even if you're on the phone) and compliment the buyer. Flattery will get you everywhere. Conflict will get you nowhere.

Step 5: sell yourself

Explain why you need a deal. It will make the salesperson feel good if he thinks he's helped you out in some way.

Step 6: get to a win-win situation to ensure you're both happy

Occasionally, I will walk away and return another day because I am not getting what I want. Don't be afraid to do the same.

TO HIT THE MONEY SPOT™
you need to become an expert negotiator. Business growth requires sales AND contracts that get you paid as quickly as possible with minimum hassle.

6

It's Time To Hone Your Sales Skills

I have always said I am going to teach my kids two skills: writing and selling. Once you can do these two things like a pro, the world is your oyster.

Selling gets a lot of bad press due to the minority of salespeople who are unethical. A real salesperson is a service provider. If for any reason you can't get your head around selling start calling it servicing.

Every time you need to make a sale, you are providing a service to someone. A service the buyer will value; the only reason a buyer would have to dislike you is if they feel you have taken advantage of them in some way. This is why in the negotiation chapter I say you have to conclude with a win-situation. Buyer and seller both have to win.

Selling is all about communicating effectively and reading people's minds.

If you have done all your branding correctly, your service or product should already look appealing to your niche.

Marketing brings awareness of your product to your target consumer. If you're selling online you will want to bring interested fans onto your mailing list so you can send them any offers or simply keep them entertained with interesting blogs and articles that keep you at the top of their minds.

Your ability to sell one-on-one will only become important when you start trying to get your products into shops. You may need or want to do it all on your own to start off with but eventually, growth will be contingent on hiring in-house or independent wholesale sales representatives.

The more the seller loves and understands their products, the easier it is to sell to other people. Good sales people are lively, engaging and bursting to relay how great their product is to someone.

The crucial thing about selling is to remember that service is superior to selling. The person giving you money is getting your wonderful and amazing product or service in return. It feels better to give than to receive so always develop your product or service to such a level that you feel it's a bargain no matter what the price.

The next most important thing is understanding the type of person you are selling to: different people like to be sold to in different ways and you need to figure out which category the person in front of you (or on the phone) falls into.

To sell effectively, figure out the buyer's end goal, how they make decisions and their temperament.

Buyer Personalities – End Goal of Buying Decision

I developed the **SECTAR** model of buyer types. When you have a buyer in front of you, the product aspects you focus on will depend on the type of buyer they are. A single person may have several buyer personalities with one dominant one.

Social Buyer – impressed by celebrity users of your product. So, above and beyond any testimonials if you say, 'Beyonce owns one,' for example, they're sold.

Ethical Buyer – very into being green.

Conspicuous Consumer – loves prestige, not only aspirational but love to show off their achievements.

Time Poor Buyer – loves convenience and ease of use. The more time you'll save them, the better.

Aspirational Buyer – likes to have better things than the average person.

Risk-averse Buyer – very concerned by safety and security issues.

Buyer Personalities – How A Decision Is Made

Fast-Decisive Buyer

Makes decisions easily provided you give them all the information they need and want. Typically this type of buyer will have done lots of research on the product before they come to buy and will become slow and impatient if they feel you're going over things they already know.

Slow-Indecisive Buyer

Finds it tough to make decisions and is very vulnerable to feeling 'I was pressured into buying this.' Don't rush this type of buyer; move at their pace.

Buyer Personalities – Temperament

Analytical Buyer

Someone with an analytical mindset is very interested in numbers and features. Statistics will please them. Ask them what they want or like and try to match the product's features with the buyer's likes.

Emotional Buyer

An emotional buyer is more interested in understanding a product's benefits rather than knowing a list of features.

A *feature* is anything that a product has or does. It is a fact that can't be disputed, e.g. Queen of Kinks shampoo doesn't contain sulfates.

A *benefit* is a utility, e.g. Queen of Kinks shampoo is mild so that it doesn't strip your hair of its good oils but still effective enough to clean real dirt and grime away properly.

TO HIT THE MONEY SPOT™
learn how to sell effectively by figuring out each unique buyer's end goals, decision-making process and their temperament

THE REAL REASONS FOR FAILURE

1

Chasing Money

It's pretty simple, if money is all there is in it for you, you're bound to fail sooner or later. I have seen one alternative to loving your product and that's loving business itself. Some people, myself included to a certain degree, just LOVE business. They love strategizing, creating and developing a framework for a business.

I arrived in Great Britain in 2002 with one suitcase. One of the things I packed was a folder full of business plans that I had written on paper during my gap year between high school and university. I just loved business and had always wanted to start one.

I was recently cleaning the files on my computer and found about 10 folders containing business ideas with fully-fledged plans. There are some businesses I would definitely enjoy running more than others but ultimately I would rather be running any business than having to be in a job with all its restrictions.

My dad is exactly the same.

He started doing business before he was even a teenager and has been running a business of one form or another throughout his life. By the time he hit his most successful business aged 32 he had tried and tested so many. He had learned he didn't enjoy employment and loved business even after coming to the brink of collapse.

Living in one of the world's poorest countries, his strategy for starting a business in the early 80s was simple. He walked around from one shop to the next, looked at the different products on offer and thought through whether or not he could make the product in question. He reasoned that the fewer the inputs, the easier it would be for him to import raw materials.

Whenever he thought he could make something, he went home and carried out more research on it. In the end, he settled on candle manufacturing. The Gods must have seen his hard work and suffering because six months later this man who had been born in a village hut and had worn patchwork shorts growing up had turned over the equivalent of GBP150,000 (c.USD250,000). This is 1983/1984 when this was worth a lot more than it is today.

Every time I hear the story I get goose bumps because through this story I feel the endless possibilities of this world.

I think if my father, with all the limitations of being born in what is still one of the 10 poorest countries in the world, could follow his passion of owning a business and achieve *that* – what excuse do I have? What excuse do you have?

TO HIT THE MONEY SPOT™
you have to be in a passion-led business or have a serious passion for business in and of itself.

2

Happily Mediocre Friends

Unless you're surrounded by similarly ambitious people you will operate below your optimal performance. In *From Good To Amazing*, Michael Serwa goes as far as to say you are the average of the five people you hang out with the most, in terms of happiness, finances, personal growth, everything.

If your friends are happy to be average they make you feel OK when you underperform; they even justify that underperformance. Mediocre people don't come out and say, *I am mediocre*, their self-limiting beliefs are evident in the things they say and do. Watch out for statements that indicate a small thinker.

Some people don't believe in their ability to achieve great things; others think success is a source of embarrassment rather than pride. You know what? Your failure and your mediocrity serve no one, least of all yourself and your family. Bill Gates, one the richest men in the world, lives very well and gives with generosity. He made his money, he enjoys it and he gives away in spades.

I recall having a debate with peers in Cambridge concerned by how the tax system seemed to penalize hard workers when one person blurted out 'Well it's your fault for getting so rich.' As though hard work that culminated in wealth was a crime or something to be ashamed of.

Another time, I was watching the TV show *Loose Women*. The few times I'd flipped past the show whilst I perused what was on, I had perceived it to be an intellectually upmarket show where women discussed pertinent issues of the day. In fact, I watched it for 10 minutes and had to change the channel because I couldn't take the sheer ridiculousness of some of the things that were being said. One lady boasted proudly that she has never bought an investment property and owned only the property she lived in. She thought buying property was greedy as evidenced by the property bubble and the credit crunch.

It may have been the same lady, perhaps not, who stated that she'd grown up in social housing but because her mother was quite an 'aspirational' woman (expressed with scorn) she opted to buy when the Thatcher Government brought in the right-to-buy social housing program. She went on to argue that her mother had disadvantaged herself in doing so because as a property owner she now can't get as many old age benefits from the government. I think this was the point when I switched programmes.

I refuse to watch anything in which hard work, wealth and aspiration are seen as negative things and leeching off the Government is viewed as a positive. Aspiration, wealth and hard work are not things to be embarrassed by. The privileged should certainly pay their fair share of taxes and give back through charity but I hate people who talk of these things as though they're dirty.

Sometimes the mediocrity of friends is revealed by the things they do rather than what they say. Take a good look at your friends; those who share nothing with you but the latest gossip are not benefitting you. Those passionate about self-development and seeking role models are positive influences.

If you discover you are surrounded by mediocrity it's time to make new friends and to start increasing your exposure to positive influences. Start with what you watch. Television is full of entrepreneurial shows and competitions: Bloomberg's *GameChangers*, *The Apprentice* – although it can get pretty fabricated, *Shark Tank* in the US, *Dragon's Den* in the UK and so the list continues.

Make new friends by joining courses or entrepreneurial meetups via entrepreneur.meetup.com.

I'm not saying dump your mediocre friends, I'm saying don't immerse yourself in their way of thinking because sooner or later it will become your way of thinking.

TO HIT THE MONEY SPOT™
surround yourself with positive thinking, ambitious friends. If you need more of those, join entrepreneurial networking groups and courses.

3

Shitty Lovers

The people we choose to make our lives with can make us or break us. The sad fact is that many choose to stay with a partner that is not supportive of their hopes and dreams. I'm not talking about physically or emotionally abusive relationships here, those are special cases.

Watch out for these five types of partners. They will hold you back:

* The hyper conservative
* The discourager
* The pessimist
* The free loader a.k.a. scrubs
* The dictator

Hyper conservative partners are very risk averse. You see opportunity, they see a huge, life-shaking risk. A very conservative partner will map out so many things that could go wrong with your plans and ideas that you will actually start to believe them. If one of their predictions is realized early into your business venture it may convince you further that they are right so you will give up. You need to have a plan for dealing with their scenarios – well, those that sound remotely likely anyway.

Hear it from me: in business, something goes wrong every day. Suck it up and march on, it's part of the fun.

The discouragers are driven by jealousy. It's not that they don't want you to do well but they are scared of you outperforming them. They too discourage you by telling you why your plan is so flawed but risk-aversion is not their driving force as with hyper conservative partners, envy is.

Nothing can zap your enthusiasm like **a pessimist**; fortunately, I've known very few of those in my life. Pessimists usually see things from a negative point of view – it's not just your business ambitions, it's everything. If you can keep your passion and drive strong despite a pessimistic lover, more power to you.

It is definitely easier to start a business when you know that your partner is in a position to help with the bills when funds are tight. However, if your partner doesn't work, is content to let you pay all the bills and is generally a **scrub** you have to hit the road without this comfort. Of all the partners who can hold you back, this one is the most benign. He will provide moral support but nothing else. You will have to stay in your day job until the business is solid because anything else would be too risky. That's OK. It may take you a little longer to hit your goals but you will get there.

Now – **the dictator**. If he doesn't believe you should start a business, this type of partner is the worst type of all five. He will make you feel that if you do go ahead, you are disobeying him and the relationship is at risk. This type of dominant personality can be driven by any number of factors: a need to control, jealousy, stinginess, fear of risk or all the above.

I would not last with a dominator. I have a friend who is married to one and has made peace with the fact that she will probably never own a business. Alternatively, you need to have a really strong character too so you can overcome opposition from a dictator.

Ultimately, the stronger your self-belief, drive and passion the less any partner will be able to hold you back. If you're still just dating, figure out what type of partner you have and if it's the wrong type, run!

Having a supportive partner will push you forward.

TO HIT THE MONEY SPOT™

figure out exactly what type of partner you have and how you will deal with the curve balls they throw in your path.

4

Perfectionist Non-Starters

Earlier I mentioned a friend who wants to buy a home as a prerequisite to starting a business and won't settle for living where she can afford to buy. Well this friend is also a bit of a perfectionist. I love her dearly and hope if she reads this book she'll be stimulated into action.

You will know by now that a blog is crucial to growing a following. My friend agreed and decided she would start a blog, but she wanted to do some solid research first because she wanted to be taken seriously. It's coming on to 18 months now and that blog has not been started.

Seriously, when it comes to writing blogs and making videos you just need to start. Shoot a video using your phone and upload it to YouTube. In fact, nowadays there are apps that allow you to record, edit and upload straight from your phone. The quality is not as good as when you use a proper camera and edit within a more developed video editor but it does the job.

I personally used YouTube's Capture app to record a vlog when my husband and I went on holiday to India and despite the poor quality our videos were well received by our fans.

If there is anything you're scared of doing, stop procrastinating, get an online tutorial and get on with it.

I have several perfectionist friends.

Another friend started telling me about his passion to start a business in 2005. It is now 2015 and he is still in a job, albeit a very high paying one. Still, every time we meet he is researching something related to starting his own enterprise. He had very few responsibilities most of the last 10 years and could have taken the risk but now that he has a one-year old baby, I very much doubt he'll ever take the bull by the horns.

The message I am trying to portray is best explained by a phrase I got from *Rework* by Jason Fried and David Heinemeier Hansson: *done is better than perfect.*

TO HIT THE MONEY SPOT™
remember that you don't
need to achieve perfection.
Perfection is not achievable.
What you need to do is
start to work consistently on
what you have started.

5

No Consistency

Consistency is my secret weapon.

Consistency took me from being a low A / high B student who came somewhere in the top 10 to the unbeatable A* student who won a full scholarship to the University of Cambridge.

Sometimes high school students ask me for tips on how I got into Cambridge; unfortunately if you're already 16 or older when you ask me, as they typically are, it's a bit late for me to relay the secret. I started studying consistently when I was 11 years old. For secondary school I went to boarding school – a few weeks late when friendships had already been formed and I found it hard to make friends.

Every term, from the beginning, I would write a timetable and spend four to five hours *daily* outside of scheduled teaching revising and doing homework. Most people only did this when exams or tests were round the corner.

I accidentally discovered two things: firstly, my grades improved each and every single term; secondly, the whole studying thing started getting easier and easier with time. My brain began to retain larger volumes of information for longer periods of time.

There were a couple of people I revered and viewed as being academically on another playing field; I decided they were unbeatable but by the end of my second year in high school I was scoring the same as them in several subjects. I was by now always first, second or third in 90% of tests.

By the time I reached the sixth and final year of school I actually *knew I* was unbeatable. No one can take away six years of hard work. I never crammed. I just followed the same strategy of consistency and it worked.

Now, why have I gone so far back into history to demonstrate this here point of consistency? Well, it's simple. When I started my business I was doing exactly the same thing.

I set a weekly schedule of goals and I stuck to it. I did some work every day and recommend you do exactly the same. You can't write five blogs in one week and none in the following week. If you commit to a certain number of marketing activities per week then you need to do all of them.

To achieve consistency don't place too much on your plate. Set yourself SMART (Specific, Measurable, Attainable,

Realistic and Time-related) goals. If you need help to remain consistent, get help.

The truth is most people can't do this one thing – remain consistent. It follows that by becoming one of those rare people who can stick to something, you're already miles ahead of the pack.

TO HIT THE MONEY SPOT™
you have to work on your business consistently. You have to do what you set yourself to do, week in, week out. If it's not working, pivot your strategy, don't just stop trying.

6

Multi-tasking

Nobody can multi-task efficiently. If you're working on one thing, you're not working on another.

When I first started my business I thought I could run three businesses at the same time. I spent some time writing blogs and making videos for each. It wasn't efficient and I wasn't seeing much growth in any business. Here are five reasons why multi-tasking will do your business more harm than good:

1 Task-switching wastes time

If you're switching between very different tasks in any one day you will probably have to spend time getting into a rhythm for each one, every time. You waste time as you move from task to task. If you are working on related tasks then there isn't much time wasted in switching your attention between tasks. If the tasks build on each other then the work done on one task will help with the completion of the next task.

For instance, on days when I will be making a How-to video I may spend the morning crafting a hair recipe or writing the related blog entry, early afternoon shooting the video and evening editing it; all different tasks but interrelated.

2 Inefficiency and lower productivity

If you multi-task by answering emails, tweets and other messages whilst you work you are slowing yourself down by a huge amount. I have no alerts on my phone except for text messages. Very few people text me nowadays so it is not a major distraction. All other apps that can send alerts and notifications including WhatsApp are set not to alert me. I know if there is a message waiting when I go to my phone. If I get a text message whilst I am working on something, it normally doesn't get answered until I am done.

When I work, I work exclusively on whatever I am working on. I don't even have emails flowing through to my mail app; they are all manually downloaded for when I decide I want to check mail.

This may sound bizarre but once you get used to it, you won't want to work any other way. It's simple. Go to every single app on your phone or iPad that alerts you when something is happening and set it to stop. Checking email only at specific times is the hardest thing to get used to but you will eventually prefer not being enslaved by emails.

When I was learning how to ignore email and to only check it periodically I had to move the mail app off the home screen of my phone. I couldn't bare to look at it and not check it every few seconds. Email controlled me as it does most people.

Once you see how much more you are getting done, it will get a lot easier.

3 More mistakes

Every brain has a limited amount of processing power. If you make it split attention across several tasks you will make more errors. Even mechanical actions are impossible when you are doing a complex task, for instance, it's hard to edit a video and manage emails simultaneously, but you can call a supplier as you walk to a meeting.

The brain can't handle writing a blog and watching TV at the same time. Don't kid yourself. Get classical music on and write your blog; TV is not your friend.

4 Higher levels of stress

Multitasking is not conducive to working in a relaxed manner. Want to cut down on stress? Don't multitask unnecessarily. I hear some of you say 'Not seeing my emails as they come in will stress me out!' No, it won't. Start off by checking your emails twice a day, say at 11.00 am after you've done your first tasks of the day and 4.00 pm after a few solid hours of afternoon work. You choose the times. If you have to check first thing in the morning then do that. The risk is that some emails may completely derail what you planned to do that morning.

Spend an hour answering all emails then shut your email down to do more work. If you don't see efficiency gains, something is very, very wrong.

5 Your subconscious works while you sleep

Have you ever struggled to find a solution to a problem, gone to bed and woken up with the answer? This is because your subconscious logs all the things you are working on and in the time you're not working it's still trying to solve the problem.

If your mind is focused on just one business or element of your business then you will incrementally get ideas to improve that area. All your ideas build on each other.

However, if you are trying to do too many things at the same time then your brain will have to split its work. When you are focused on one thing the other will suffer. You will have more eureka moments related to whatever your current focus is and less on any other.

For inspiration on the benefits of focus read *The One Thing* by Gary Keller and Jay Papasan.

TO HIT THE MONEY SPOT™
focus only on one business
and only on one thing at
any moment in time.

7

The Lack Of An Accountability Buddy Or Coach

Show me a successful person and I will show you someone who was accountable to someone else to reach their heights of success.

It doesn't matter what field you choose: sport, weight loss or business, accountability is a crucial factor in succeeding. You need to be accountable to someone other than yourself. An objective third-party is the best accountability partner you can have.

Many studies have confirmed that when you are accountable to someone else for achieving specific written goals, you become more likely to succeed.

Eighteen months into running my hair product business, I was fortunate enough to realize that if I was going to grow I needed to expand my network. I started joining business networking groups and in the process found myself a buddy.

How do you find a buddy?

The more networking events you attend, the more likely you are to find someone you click with. They don't have to be in the same industry as you, in fact, it might be better if they are not.

How do you work with an accountability buddy?

Each of you needs to write Specific, Measurable, Attainable, Realistic and Time-related (SMART) goals that you share with each other. This way, you know what the other is trying to achieve.

Then meet or video chat at least weekly to discuss how you are doing. Weekly is ideal. A month is too long a stretch of time to stay unaccountable.

You can start your journey of accountability with some coaching so you know how to plan and grow but over the long haul you need someone else to be accountable to. Coaches charge by the hour, accountability buddies are meant to be free because the payment is an exchange of services, being accountable to each other to grow and develop.

A buddy is meant to be a long-term mutually-beneficial relationship. It requires an investment of time, say, 30 to 60 minutes per week, in order to work.

TO HIT THE MONEY SPOT™
find and commit to
working with an
accountability buddy for
the long term. The return
on that investment of
time is phenomenal.

SO LONG, FAREWELL

We've pretty much covered all the bases so, what are you going to do with all this knowledge? Implementation is everything. You can either try to do everything by yourself or get help doing some things to save time and accelerate the process.

Everyone has ideas.

The homeless guy you just passed on the street, he has business ideas too – possibly every day. Ideas are one of the most useless things on earth. Action and implementation is where all the value lies. The difference between progress and no progress is action.

Take action, now, today.

To give you a headstart, I have two great offers for you:

1 Go to katsonga.com and grab my latest freebie on the home page.
2 Even better, if you review this book on Amazon and send a link of the review to info@nenonatural.com, I'll let you borrow my brain for free. So I don't miss the email the subject should be 'Phone Me Now'
   * Include your Amazon review and phone number in the email.

* I'll give you a 15-minute call
* During this 15-minute phone call I will answer your three biggest business worries. Now there's an offer you won't get anywhere else.

To your roaring success.

THE AUTHOR

Heather refers to herself as a stay-at-home-working-mum; it's a hybrid of the stay-at-home mum and the working mum. *Why choose when you can have both?*

After graduating with First Class Honours in Economics from the University of Cambridge, she spent seven years in investment banking – first at Goldman Sachs then at HSBC. Despite the 6-figure income, however, she was unacceptably time poor; she wanted **both** money *and* a life.

So, she sat down, wrote a plan for getting out of the banking industry and into the more flexible, less stressful life she craved. It didn't work out to plan, it was better than she could have ever imagined!

Her first business – coaching people on how to get into investment banking as girlbanker.com – wasn't as exciting as she'd imagined it would be so she swiveled and started a product business.

Heather's been interested in running a business from the time she was a teenager but she always 'knew' she would hate anything that involved selling physical products. She was wrong, many of her fears, most of them regarding how complicated and involving it would be, were unfounded.

Having gone from, 'I would never run a product business' to 'product businesses are *where it's at!'* she decided to get everything she had learned on paper. By the time she was done she'd designed a business model, *The Money Spot*™ Framework, a tested roadmap for earning more money and living a full life. She had to share it.

Heather still sells products; she's behind the very popular dry hair product line, *Queen of Kinks, Curls & Coils*®, so she splits her working time between running her product business and teaching people how to build their own product business.

In her spare time Heather plays mum, wife and YouTube life vlogger.

Printed in Great Britain
by Amazon